Spreadsheets, The Easy Way

by Paul Bocij

ISBN 07457 0076 4

Kuma

Spreadsheets, The Easy Way

Published by:

Kuma Computers Ltd
12 Horseshoe Park
Pangbourne
Berks
RG8 7JW

Tel 0734 844335
Fax 0734 844339

About This Book

All examples and illustrations are based on AsEasyAs and AsEasyAs Lite from TRIUS Incorporated. The illustrations were captured from the program in a number of ways. For screen shots, several Shareware and Public Domain utilities were used to capture the screen as a text file or .PCX graphics file. Worksheets were prepared by printing them to disk in landscape format and then editing the resulting ASCII file.

Dedication

In memory of my father, who genuinely thought that all technology - especially computers - was "witchcraft".

Acknowledgements

TRIUS Incorporated for permission to base this book upon their spreadsheet products.

Steve Lee and Shareware Publishing for their friendly support.

Jon Day and Tim Moore of Kuma Computers for their assistance and support.

Lin Mellor, senior IT lecturer at the University of Derby, and Graham Templeman, senior Finance lecturer at the University of Derby, for their assistance during the production of this book.

The University of Derby and Nottingham University for access to information and resources.

My wife, Helen, for her help during the first draft.

Trademarks

Contents

Section 1: Introduction

1.1 What is a spreadsheet?

Imagine a sales ledger with a list of customers on one side and row of figures on the other. Each time a sale is recorded, the name of the customer and the value of the transaction is written in by hand. At the end of the month, all of the sales are added together and the total is used in a number of other calculations to maintain the company's accounts system. If the company makes a substantial number of sales each month, maintaining the sales ledger will become very expensive in terms of time, effort and money.

Now, imagine that all of the information in the sales ledger can be held in an electronic form by a computer. Instead of working through each entry by hand at the end of the month, we can now simply give the computer an order along the lines of: "if it is the end of the month, add up all of the lines in the sales ledger and display the total". The whole process becomes automatic and is performed within a matter of seconds. Some of the huge amount of time and labour that has been saved can now be invested in *using* the information in the sales ledger to improve the company's position. For example, the entries in the sales ledger can be analysed to give information on areas such as demand trends and customer buying patterns.

This is what a spreadsheet is: a program designed to store and manipulate values, numbers and text in an efficient and useful way.

The work area in a spreadsheet program is called the WORKSHEET. A worksheet is a grid made up of CELLS. Each cell is uniquely identifiable by its horizontal (ROW) and vertical (COLUMN) co-ordinates. A cell can contain text, numbers or a formula that relates to information held in another cell. For example, a cell could contain any of these pieces of data:

127
"Cash Flow Forecast"
+A12 (a reference to another cell)

The diagram below shows how a worksheet is organised. Cell co-ordinates are traditionally given in the form of row-column. For example, the very first cell in a worksheet is A1. Most spreadsheets can have worksheets measuring hundreds of cells. AsEasyAs Lite, for example, has a maximum worksheet size of 2,048 rows by 128 columns, giving a total of 262,144 cells. To cope with such large widths, rows follow a numbering system like this: A...Z, AA...AZ, BA...BZ, CA...CZ and so on.

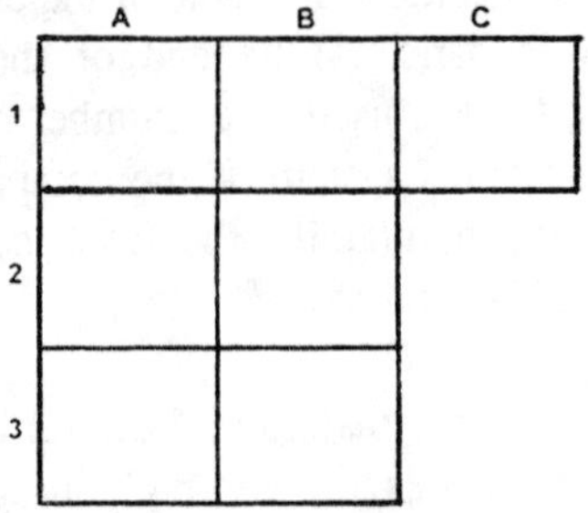

In other words, if we were to move horizontally across the top row of the worksheet, the co-ordinates we moved through would be A1, B1, C1, D1 and so on. After reaching Z1, the numbering system would alter slightly, continuing from AA1, AB2, AC3 and so on. After AZ1 would come BA1, BA2, etc.

1.2 Automatic recalculation.

The most important feature of a spreadsheet is its ability to update the entire worksheet each time a change is made. For example, imagine that the cell at A1 contains information based on the contents of the cell at B1. Changing the contents of B1 causes the computer to update the worksheet, placing a new value in A1 automatically.

Using some real numbers might help to make this a little clearer. Imagine that B1 contains the number 12 and A1 contains a formula to the effect of "take whatever is in B1 and add 6 to it". Using this formula, the result contained in A1 would be 18. Now, changing B1 so that it contained 20 would cause A1 to change too, giving a new result of 26.

Spreadsheets also have the ability to modify the relationships made between cells. Using the above example again, imagine now that the contents of both A1 and B1 are moved to C1 and D1 respectively. When the worksheet is updated, C1 will now automatically obtain its data from D1 because the formula would have changed from "take whatever is in B1 and add 6 to it" to "take whatever is in D1 and add 6 to it". In the example, the program would have altered the relationship given in the formula to match the change made in the worksheet. There are other ways of altering the relationships made between cells but these will be explored a little later on.

If all of this seems a little obscure, it will become clearer during the practical exercises that follow in later sections.

1.3 Why use a spreadsheet?

Perhaps the simplest way to describe the value of a spreadsheet is to suggest that it allows users to concentrate on the results themselves instead of the way they are produced. For management, a spreadsheet is a *primary decision support system*, collating and processing data to create information. The words "data" and "information" have very different meanings when we discuss decision support and related areas. A good way to illustrate this is by saying that "data" means raw facts whilst "information" means data that has been processed so that it is meaningful (to the person who receives it). The diagram below should make this clearer.

Data

We have 5 tons of steel in stock
1 ton of steel makes 8,000 knives
We produce and sell 20,000 knives each month

Information

We have sufficient stocks to last 2 months

Unlike a printed report, a worksheet is fluid and can reflect probabilities as well as absolutes. The major benefits of a spreadsheet can be summarised as follows:

* Ease of use, giving reductions in time and labour. A spreadsheet removes entirely the need to perform calculations manually. Amendments to a worksheet take effect almost immediately and are automatically posted to every other part of spreadsheet.

* Repetitive tasks, such as the production of monthly statements, can be simplified by using standard templates or customised applications.

* Standardisation. Templates and other methods can be used to standardise the way in which work is carried out and the way the results are presented.

* Accuracy. Providing the worksheet has been constructed properly, the computer guarantees accuracy in all calculations.

* Simulation. Even the most complex situations can be represented by a worksheet model.

* Modelling. The speed and flexibility of a spreadsheet program allow "what if?" questioning to be carried out.

1.4 Choosing a spreadsheet.

The standard for all major spreadsheet packages is based on a program called Lotus 1-2-3, first launched in 1982 and renowned as the world's best selling package. The most distinctive feature of the program is its command system which uses "hot keys" and a series of menus accessed by the "/" key. Most spreadsheets offer at least limited compatibility with 1-2-3's command system and file format. Some packages, like early versions of AsEasyAs, are almost identical to the original and are sold upon this basis. Even the popularity of Microsoft's Windows environment has done little to change the popularity of Lotus lookalikes. Windows applications like Excel have managed to retain the full Lotus command system alongside their own control routines.

Amongst the most popular spreadsheet packages on the market, the following offer at least limited compatibility with the Lotus 1-2-3 standard: PC Planner, Excel, Quattro, SuperCalc and AsEasyAs, AsEasyAs Lite (ALite).

Owners of IBM-compatible machines might be interested in packages designed to run in the Windows environment. These are generally considered to be the easiest to use, particularly since all Windows applications contain extensive on-line help facilities. Unfortunately, Windows packages tend to be quite expensive and are almost certain to be out of reach for certain groups, such as students.

By far the two most important features to look for in a spreadsheet package are:

* Compatibility with the Lotus 1-2-3 command system.

* File import and export facilities for Lotus .WKS and .WK1 worksheet files.

If the prices of some of the programs mentioned above are prohibitive, it might be worthwhile looking for a cut-down version of each program or examining the Public Domain and Shareware market. For example, Lotus 1-2-3 Go! is aimed especially at beginners to spreadsheets and retails for less than half the price of the full version. In the Shareware market, although the registration fee for AsEasyAs is already remarkably low, a reduced version, AsEasyAs Lite, can be registered for less than the price of a box of good quality blank disks.

Owners of other machines, such as the Atari STE or Commodore Amiga, will find that comparable programs are a little cheaper than their PC counterparts, although there is likely to be far less variety. Unfortunately, the same is also true of the Shareware markets for these kinds of machines.

1.5 Hardware requirements.

Almost any computer is capable of running a spreadsheet program. A basic PC compatible with 256K of memory, a single-sided disk drive and a CGA graphics card should be able to cope with the oldest versions of almost every major program on the market.

Of course, this will not apply to Windows programs or the latest versions of the most popular packages, many of which will have been enhanced beyond the basic features of Lotus 1-2-3. Even a relatively small Windows package will require approximately 5Mb of hard drive space and will perform best with a minimum of a 386SX processor.

Contrary to popular belief, a fast processor or a co-processor are not essential for working with spreadsheets. High resolution graphics allow complex graphs to be displayed but are unimportant for the bulk of most spreadsheet work. However, a graphics printer is essential for reports, particularly if you want to use compressed print or plot graphs.

As a guide to the kind of equipment needed to run a relatively sophisticated package, the minimum requirements for AsEasyAs version 5.01 are offered:

MS-DOS version 2.11
384K RAM
1 floppy disk drive (720K minimum)
Monochrome monitor

Of course, the working environment can enhanced somewhat by having access to the following:

Windows version 3.0 or higher
EMS memory installed
Hard disk drive
Mouse
VGA graphics card and monitor
Epson, Okidata or HP Laserjet II compatible printer

1.6 Installing and activating a spreadsheet.

Most packages come with their own installation routines and these will be documented in the program's manual. The usual procedure is to locate a file with a name of "INSTALL" or "SETUP" and to call this from the MS-DOS command line or Windows File Manager. These files can be identified by their extensions, usually ".EXE", ".COM" or ".BAT".

To install a program from MS-DOS, the following procedure is usually adopted:

* Start the machine as normal

* Insert the first installation disk in the floppy disk drive (usually the A:\ drive)

* Type "A" followed by a colon and press the Enter key

* Type "DIR /P" followed by Enter and examine the directory listing to identify the name of the installation program

* Type "INSTALL" or "SETUP" (depending on the name of the installation program) and press Enter

To install a program from the Windows File Manager program, the following procedure is usually adopted:

* Start Windows as normal and activate the File Manager

* Click on the A:\ disk drive button and examine the directory listing to identify the name of the installation program

* Double-click on the name of the installation program

Once the installation program begins, it should automatically copy all of the required files to a work disk or an empty sub directory on the hard disk. If the program files are compressed, it may be necessary to have access to an archiving utility, such as LHARC or PKZIP. However, most compressed programs are stored as self-extracting archive files or are supplied with the necessary extraction program.

Once all of the files have been copied into the correct location, you may be asked to supply some basic information about your computer system. This will normally concern the monitor you are using, a location where data files can be stored and information about your printer. If the program does not contain a set of standard printer drivers, you will need to enter a set of printer control codes manually although this need not be done immediately. If you are using a Windows program, it will not be necessary to enter monitor and printer information as the program will use the defaults already installed in Windows.

Windows programs will usually create their own Program Groups, allowing the spreadsheet program to be activated by simply double-clicking on its icon.

If the program has been installed as an MS-DOS application within Windows, you will need to add a new Program Item to one of your Program Groups. In Windows 3.1, this can be done as follows:

* Activate the Program Group window you wish to add the new program to

* Click on the "File" menu in Program Manager and select "New"

* A "New Program Object" dialogue box should now be on the screen. Use the mouse to check "Program Item" if it is not already highlighted and then press Enter or click on "OK"

* A new "Program Item Properties" dialogue box will appear and a cursor will be located on the "Description" line. Type in a suitable description and press Enter.

* Select "Browse" and navigate through the file system until you find the program you wish to associate with the new icon. Highlight the file's name and press Enter. The "Command Line" section in the dialogue box should now contain the path and file name for the new entry.

* If an icon shape does not appear in a corner of the dialogue box, you can select one from the set built-in to Windows by clicking on the "Change Icon" button. Ignore any dialogue box that appears telling you that there is no icon associated with the program. Select a new icon with the mouse and then click on the "OK" button.

* Click on the "OK" button in the "Program Item Properties" box to install the new Program Item.

With MS-DOS, to start the program from the hard drive, the following procedure is normally used:

* Locate the name of the sub directory where the program is stored

* Type *CD\sub directory* name to enter the sub directory

* Use the DIR command to locate the main program file

* Type the first part of the program's name (the extension is not required)

For example, AsEasyAs might be activated using the commands shown below:

```
C:
CD\ASEASYAS
ASEASY
```

Section 2: About the Exercises.

2.1 The software.

All screen shots and sample exercises were produced using AsEasyAs and AsEasyAs Lite from TRIUS Incorporated. Different versions of the these programs were used but all of the exercises have been designed to work with any version of AsEasyAs.

Full details of how to obtain these programs are contained in Appendix 1.

2.2 Differences between spreadsheet programs.

In some cases, there may be slight differences between the commands illustrated using AsEasyAs and the package you are using. However, the principles behind each procedure will be exactly the same, regardless of the specific spreadsheet program you are using. If potential problems are not highlighted in the text, there are two simple methods of dealing with them. The first is to activate the program's on-line help function, which is done by pressing F1 at any point in the program. The second is to use the reference guide supplied with most programs or refer to any other documentation you may have.

Most of the differences you will encounter will be on a cosmetic level only. For example, in the File menu, you may come across "Store" or "Save" as the command to save a worksheet to disk. In this case, both commands will obviously perform the same function and both will be activated by the same key press. Note. however, that macros may need to be modified slightly in order for them to function correctly. For example, it might be necessary to make changes alonmg the lines of substituting "S" (for "Store") in place of "F" (for "File").

A second example can be provided by examining the different graphics facilities of the various programs on the market. The pictures below show two graphs created with exactly the same data. Overall, the graphs are identical to one another but there are a number of minor differences, such as in the fill patterns and text styles.

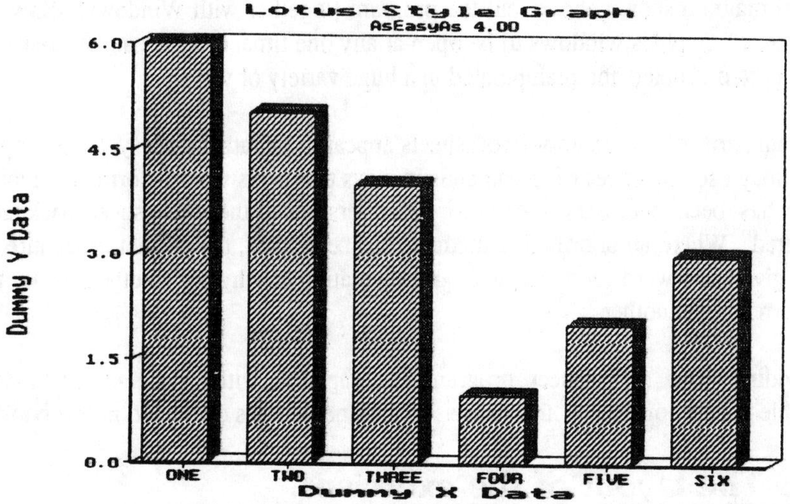
Lotus-Style Graph
AsEasyAs 4.00
6.0
4.5
3.0
1.5
0.0
Dummy Y Data
ONE
TWO
THREE
FOUR
FIVE
SIX
Dummy X Data

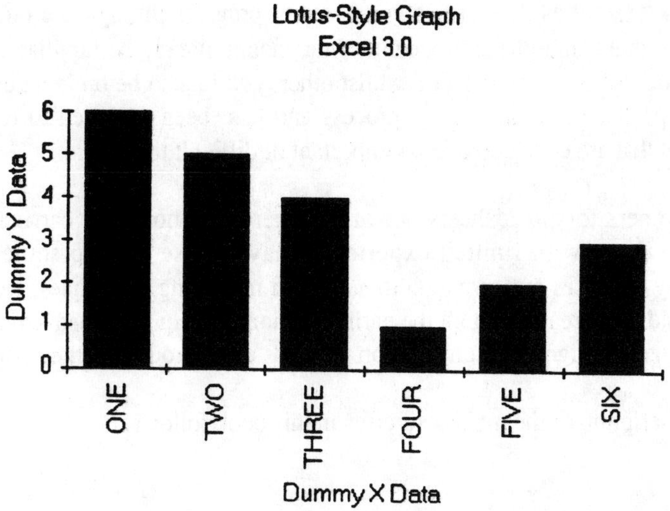
Lotus-Style Graph
Excel 3.0
6
5
4
3
2
1
0
Dummy Y Data
ONE
TWO
THREE
FOUR
FIVE
SIX
Dummy X Data

You should also take account of the fact that although all of the programs described in this book share a number of common features, some contain highly advanced facilities that can not be described in this book. It is not clear in the Excel diagram shown above, but the program (together with Windows) allows a number of graphics windows to be open at any one time. Graphs can be re-sized, cut, pasted, copied and manipulated in a huge variety of ways.

Certain parts of the example worksheets appear to be rather clumsy, for example they may use sequences of commands in ways that users would normally avoid. This has been necessary to cater for older versions of the spreadsheet packages covered. Where an unorthodox method has been used, the correct procedure is also given afterwards, together with an explanation of why one method is to be preferred over another.

Providing your spreadsheet program is compatible with Lotus 1-2-3, you will be able to carry out all of the exercises and procedures contained in this book.

2.3 The layout of the exercises.

Each exercise begins with an overview of the skills and concepts you should have gained by the end of the exercise. At the end of each session, a summary of the areas covered is given to refresh your memory. The exercises are described in stages, using step-by-step instructions to allow you to recreate the example worksheets exactly as they are shown. As you progress through the book, you will notice that some of the procedures you should already be familiar with are no longer described in great detail, whilst others continue to be broken down into simple steps. This is a deliberate process and has been designed to reinforce those skills that are considered to be important or difficult to acquire.

For newcomers to spreadsheets, all of the exercises should be carried out in sequence. Users with limited experience may choose to skip some of the preliminary exercises and move on to advanced modelling techniques. However, they should still read through the earlier sections to acquaint themselves with the worksheet design and construction methods used.throughout the book.

A brief description of the major exercises in this book follows:

1. Familiarisation

A worksheet is not created, but the user is allowed to experiment with the program, learning how to move around the worksheet, access the on-line help facility, use command menus, enter data and edit the contents of cells.

2. Car Expenses

A simple worksheet is created containing only two columns of data and a single calculation. This continues the familiarisation process and adds a number of basic skills that are essential for creating more complex worksheets. The new skills learned include erasing a worksheet from memory, defining cell ranges, copying cells, entering formulas, moving cells and saving data to disk.

3. Cash Flow Forecast 1

This worksheet continues to build upon the skills learned so far and begins to focus on aspects of design. After completing this exercise, readers should be capable of creating worksheets for a large variety of common applications. The techniques learned so far can be applied to tasks ranging from balancing a chequebook to creating a cash flow forecast for presentation to others. Apart from introducing several important design techniques, a range of new skills are presented including calculations, editing text, copying values, fixing absolute co-ordinates and formatting labels.

4. Graphics and Random Numbers

A simple worksheet is constructed that allows a variety of graphs to be created and displayed. Reports and keyboard macros are also introduced at this stage. The final part of the exercise combines the use of these new techniques in a practical demonstration of how graphs and reports can be used to supplement existing information. Sections on design and analysis show how even relatively simple worksheets can be used to diagnose business problems and produce extremely sophisticated forecasts.

6. Cash Flow Forecast 2

A sophisticated worksheet is created based on the skills and knowledge gained through earlier exercises. Some of the more advanced features of the model include Monte Carlo analysis, automatic report generation and a data entry section that can be used to interrogate the model for "what if?" questioning. The process of building upon analysis and design skills continues throughout the exercise. On completion of this exercise, users should be capable of producing worksheets to degree level.

7. Database Exercises

The more advanced features of the spreadsheet program are explored with a series of extremely short examples and exercises. Some of the areas covered include creating simple databases, generating tables, goalseeking, sorting data, carrying out searches and 3D modelling.

2.4 Concepts and analysis.

The structure of this book allows concepts and techniques to be introduced only when they are needed. In this way, unnecessary confusion is avoided and each concept can be demonstrated in the context of a practical exercise.

For reference purposes, the index allows readers to find the exact location of key terms in the body of the text.

Analysis is carried out during the course of each exercise. Reading the text concerning the exercises will give readers the necessary conceptual framework to be able to interpret and analyse most spreadsheet models.

2.5 Progression through the book.

This book has been designed to lead almost any reader from a simple worksheet containing only one calculation to a complete financial model,using sophisticated techniques such as macros, data entry screens, summary reports and Monte Carlo Analysis (simulating the effect of random events). No previous experience of spreadsheets is assumed and readers should expect to achieve the following after working through all of the exercises:

* Small businessmen should be capable of constructing cash flow forecasts to present to investors, or create simple models to help with bookkeeping procedures.

* Non-financial professionals, such as managers and intending managers, should be able to interpret and analyse intelligently almost any model presented to them, understanding the strengths and limitations of the techniques used.

* Students, including Business Studies students to undergraduate level, should be able to design and construct accurate models for course works.

* Other non-financial users should learn many of the skills described above, gaining the necessary expertise to create models to a professional standard.

The nature of examination courses makes it impossible to tailor the contents of this book towards any specific qualification. However, CNAA and university Business Studies degree-level courses tend to contain a number of common elements and these are reflected here.

Section 3: Introducing the Spreadsheet.

3.1 Objective

This chapter is intended to familiarise readers with the program's main display and to introduce a set of basic editing and movement commands. The skills gained in this section and Section 4 will allow readers to inspect and construct simple worksheets. All commands are based upon version 4.0 of AsEasyAs since this is closest to the traditional spreadsheet control system. Users of Alite, versions 5.0 and 5.1 of AsEasyAs and other programs should refer to their program manuals for details of additional features such as mouse support.

3.2 The screen display.

When the program first loads, the screen display will appear as shown. Take a few moments to become familiar with the different sections of the display.

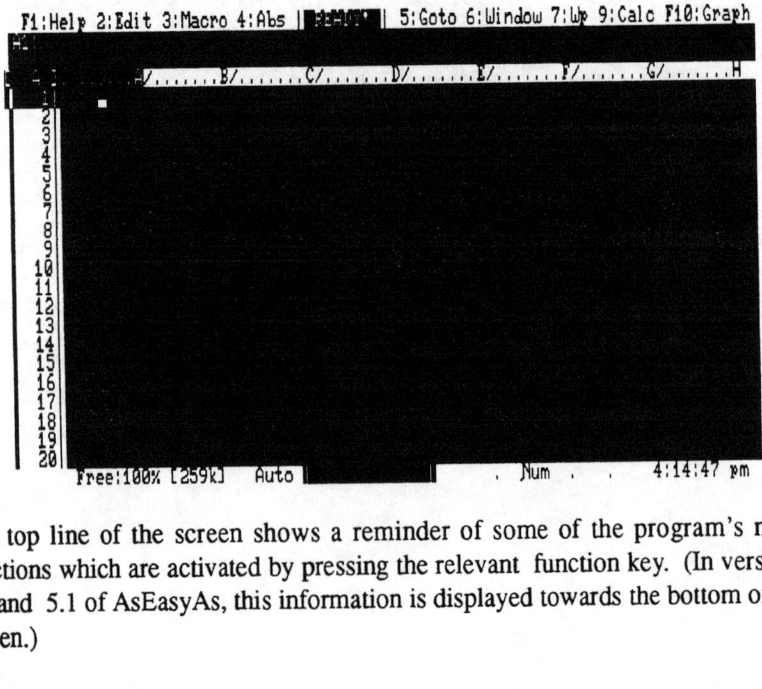

The top line of the screen shows a reminder of some of the program's main functions which are activated by pressing the relevant function key. (In versions 5.0 and 5.1 of AsEasyAs, this information is displayed towards the bottom of the screen.)

Briefly, the main functions performed by these keys are:

* F1 - Help. This calls up a comprehensive help menu.
* F2 - Edit. This allows the contents of a cell to be edited.
* F3 - Macro. This controls the execution of macros.
* F4 - Absolute. This marks a cell reference as being an absolute value.
* F5 - Goto. Allows users to move directly to any given cell in the worksheet.
* F6 - Window. Toggles between windows.
* F7 - Wp. Allows simple text editing on the screen.
* F8 - Unused.
* F9 - Calc. Recalculates the entire spreadsheet or a given range of cells.
* F10 - Graph. Displays a graph.

Detailed explanations of the terms used in these descriptions are given in later sections.

The top line of the display will also display a "READY" message, which signifies when the program has completed an operation and is ready for further instructions.

The next line of the display, marked with A1:, is a status line that is used to display and edit the contents of the current cell. As you move around the spreadsheet this line will change to display the co-ordinate of the current cell together with any number, text or formula it contains. Whenever the spreadsheet program starts, the current cell is always set to A1.

The current cell position is shown by highlighting the row and column co-ordinates on the lines that frame the worksheet area. The cell itself is highlighted in red and contains a small cursor.

The bottom line of the screen displays:

* The amount of available memory taken up by the current worksheet (as a percentage of all free memory)

* The total amount of memory available for a worksheet (in Kilobytes)

* Whether or not automatic recalculation of the worksheet is enabled (the default is "Auto")

* Keyboard status (Caps Lock, Scroll Lock, Number Lock etc.)

* The current time

3.3 Activating the help function.

To call up the help function, press F1 at any point in the program. When help is activated, the display changes to show a contents list on the left hand side of the screen and the help text on the right hand side of the screen. The cursor (arrow) keys allow you to move around the index and read any of the help text.

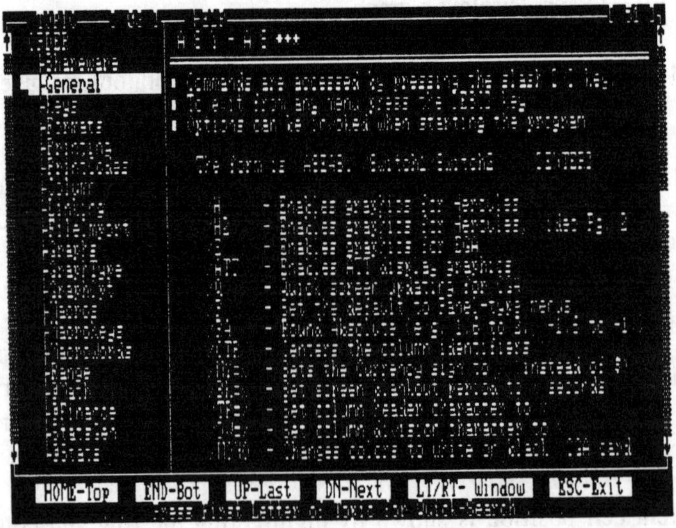

The right key (⇒) activates the help text window, allowing you to move up and down through each of the help pages on a particular topic.

The left key (⇐) activates the index window, so that you can move up and down the contents list.

The up key (⇑) scrolls up one line at a time.

The down key (⇓) scrolls down one line at a time.

In the index, Home and End will move you to the first and last entries respectively. You may also press the first letter of the subject you want to read about to move directly into that area of the index.

In both the index and the help text, you can move up and down one page at a time by using the Page Up and Page Down keys.

To leave the help function at any time, press the Escape (Esc) key.

3.4 Moving around the worksheet.

Experiment with moving around the worksheet by using the following keys.

* Left arrow - Moves left by one cell.

* Right arrow - Moves right by one cell.

* Up arrow - Moves up by one cell.

* Down arrow - Moves down by one cell.

* Page Down - Moves down by 20 cells.

* Page Up - Moves up by 20 cells.

* Tab (or Control and right arrow) - Moves right by one page.

* Shift and Tab (or Control and left arrow) - Moves left one page.

* Home - Returns to the HOME position on the screen, cell co-ordinate A1.

* End - When this is pressed, the word "End" will appear at the bottom of the screen, signifying that a block operation is about to take place. When one of the cursor keys is pressed, it will move the user to end of the current block in the direction indicated by the arrow. For example, if a block of cells extends from A1 (top left) to K20 (bottom right), End followed by the right arrow key would move to K1. Similarly, End followed by the down arrow key would move to A20.

* GOTO - When F5 is pressed, you can enter a cell co-ordinate to move to automatically.

In versions 5.0 and 5.1 of AsEasyAs, a mouse may be used to move around the worksheet. Pressing the left button will cause the current cell to become active and the right button will summon the main command menu.

3.5 Entering data into a cell.

Any kind of data can be entered into any of the cells in the worksheet. For the moment, we will ignore formulas and formatting commands and concentrate on how numbers and text are entered.

To enter any kind of text, simply type the characters required. As you type, each character will be displayed on the status line at the top of the screen (see 3.2) When you have finished, press ENTER and the text will appear inside the current cell. Any kind of text in a worksheet is referred to as a LABEL.

If the text appears to be far too long to fit into the cell, don't worry - nothing is wrong. Although the width of a cell on the screen is set to a default of 9 characters, the cell itself is capable of holding more than 200 characters at a time (typically, 255). If the cells to the left of the text are empty, the program takes the opportunity to display as much of the text as possible.

Numbers are entered in exactly the same way as text; simply type the required figures and then press ENTER. For the time being, if you want to begin a label with a number, use a single quote (') to precede the number.

If the number you attempt to type in is larger than the width of the cell, it will be displayed as a row of asterisks (*). This means only that although the number has been assigned to the cell correctly, the program is unable to display all of the digits. A later section describes how cell widths can be altered to rectify this.

3.6 Editing the contents of a cell.

To edit a cell, position the cursor over it and press the F2 key. You will now find that the display line at the top of the screen can be edited. The cursor keys can be used to move along the line and the following keys can also be used:

* Home - move to the beginning of the line.

* End - move to the end of the line.

* Delete - erase the character to the right of the cursor.

* Backspace (←) - erase the character to the left of the cursor.

* Insert - toggle between Insert and Overwrite modes. In Overwrite mode, new characters delete those already present at the cursor position.

After the line has been edited, pressing ENTER writes the changed data back to the cell and the worksheet is updated. An editing operation can be aborted without changing the contents of the cell by pressing the ESCAPE key twice.

3.7 Using the command menu.

The main command menu is accessed by pressing the "/" key which is located to the right of the space bar. The picture below shows how the main menu appears.

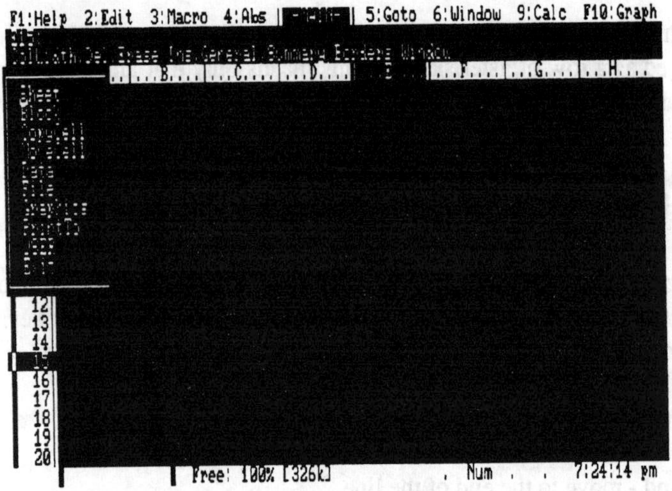

There are two different ways of choosing a menu item. The first is by using the menu bar, which is controlled by the following keys:

* Left arrow, up arrow or Backspace - move the menu bar up
* Right arrow, down arrow or Space - move the menu bar down
* ENTER - make the selection

The second method is by simply pressing the key corresponding to the (highlighted) first letter of the item required. In this way, commands can be abbreviated to a brief set of key presses. For example, "/GOTF" would be a shorthand way of describing how to enter the main title of a graph and could be broken down into the following steps:

* / - Activate the command (main) menu
* G - Move into the Graph sub menu
* O - Move into the Options sub menu
* T - Move into the Titles sub menu

* F - Select First Title

It is possible to backtrack through each menu level by pressing the ESCAPE key repeatedly. Pressing ESCAPE from the main menu returns you to the worksheet.

Try the example above to see how the menu system works. Use the ESCAPE key so that you do not need to enter a graph title (although it is not important if you do).

For the sake of convenience, many of the procedures detailed later on will use the shorthand method described here.

3.8 Summary

In this section, you have learned how to:

* Move around the worksheet

* View the contents of a cell

* Access command menus

* Use the on-line help facility

* Enter data into cells

* Edit the contents of a cell

Section 4: The First Worksheet

4.1 Objective

In this chapter, we build a simple worksheet model containing only a single calculation. Despite the simplicity of the model, a wide range of new editing and presentation features are introduced, building upon the material already covered.

4.2 Erasing a worksheet from memory.

If the spreadsheet program is already running, you may wish to clear the contents of the current worksheet before starting the next exercise.

To erase the current worksheet, carry out the following steps:

* Call up the main menu by pressing the "/" key

* The first entry, *Worksheet*, is already highlighted, so just press enter to move into the Worksheet sub-menu

* Move the menu bar to the option marked "Erase" and press Enter

* The program will now ask you to confirm whether or not the current worksheet in memory should be deleted. Highlight "Yes" and press Enter.

An alternative way of performing the steps above would be to press the following keys in order: /, W, E, Y. In the shorthand form discussed in Section 3, this would be presented as "/WEY".

4.3 Creating the sample worksheet.

This first exercise builds a simple worksheet that calculates the cost of running a car for one year. Estimated expenses are listed in a single column and added together to give a final total.

Enter the data below into the relevant cells of the worksheet (cell co-ordinates are given on the left). If you are unsure about how to enter text or numbers into a cell, refer to section 3.5.

```
A4... Road Tax
A5... Insurance
A6... MOT
A7... Services
A8... Repairs
A9... Fuel
A11... Total:

B4... 100
B5... 150
B6... 75
B7... 150
B8... 225
B9... 750
```

The worksheet should now appear as in the diagram below.

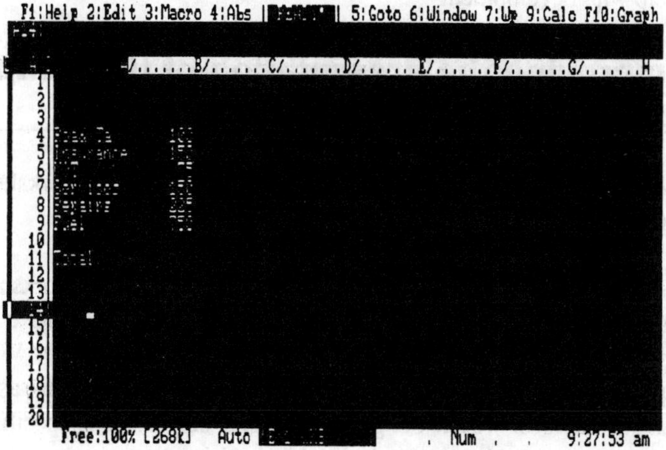

The appearance of the worksheet leaves a lot to be desired. Imagine the confusion you would feel if you were a stranger looking at the model. How would you interpret the different areas of the worksheet? For example, is the row marked "Total:" the sum of the items above, or is it some other kind of expense? Although you could reasonably expect someone to make a set of intelligent assumptions about the worksheet, this would not be possible with larger models.

4.4 Improving presentation.

We can make models more understandable by using three simple techniques:

* Titles - each section of a model should contain a meaningful title that describes the purpose of that area of the model.

* Spacing - the worksheet area is large enough so that even huge models can be presented to users in manageable sections. With a little careful planning, it is possible to design the layout of the worksheet so that users are only presented with the information they need. For example, management staff should not have to wade through hundreds of calculations in order to obtain a simple total; far better to devote an area of the worksheet specifically to this.

* Notes - these can be used to help someone understand the model or to help with development.

4.5 Improving the presentation of the sample worksheet (1).

Let's use the techniques described above to make the sample worksheet a little more presentable.

The first thing that needs to be done is to add a title to the worksheet. Move to B1 and enter "Car Expenses" as a label. Below this, in B2, enter a line of 12 minus signs preceded by a single quote ('). Do the same in B10. Without the single quote, the program would attempt to treat the minus signs as part of a formula and an error would be generated. The single quote specifies that the data that follows should be treated as a label. Using the single quote again enter a line of 12 equality signs into B12.

The worksheet should now appear as shown below.

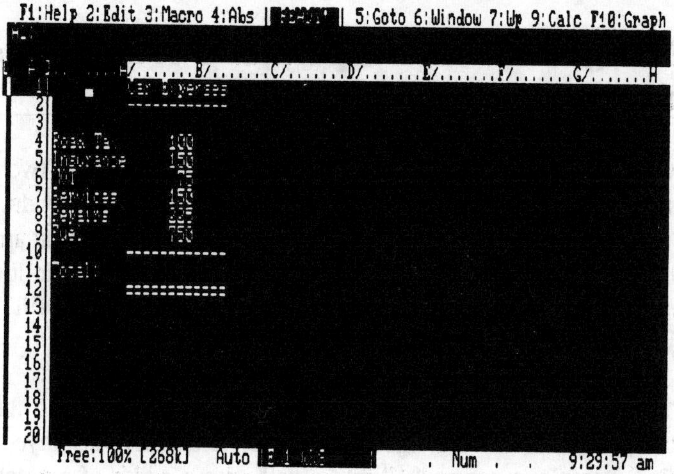

We can still improve on this a little, by using a few more of the program's built-in facilities.

4.6 Formatting labels.

It was mentioned a little earlier that the single quote (') could be used to precede numbers to specify that they be treated as a label. However, apart from specifying the existence of a label, the single quote also serves to instruct the program to display the contents of the cell *left aligned* (sometimes also called left justified). In other words, this character formats the contents of the cell so that the left margin is flush with the left edge of the cell. Two other characters can be used to format the contents of a cell on other ways. The "^" character *centres* the contents of the cell and the double quote (") *right justifies* the contents of the cell. To summarise this for reference purposes:

* ' - Left justify (left align) the contents of a cell (this is the default for all labels)

* ^ - Centre the contents of a cell

* " - Right justify (right align) the contents of a cell

4.7 Filling a cell with repetitions of the same character

Earlier, we underlined sections of the worksheet by using a line of twelve minus signs or twelve equality signs. You should have noticed that the width of each column was set to nine characters (the default) and so we had what appeared to be an "overspill" of three characters into the next column. It follows that if we were to make the column width bigger, the line would no longer fill the entire width of the cell and would have to be extended manually.

The "\" command fills a cell with the character that follows it. If the column width is adjusted, so too are the number of characters displayed on the screen. For example, entering "*" into a cell with a width of nine characters, would display a line of nine asterisks on the screen. If the column width were to be changed to 25 characters, then the command would adjust the cell so that it now displayed 25 asterisks.

4.8 Improving the presentation of the worksheet (2).

We can now apply some more of these techniques to the sample worksheet.

Move to cell A10 and enter "\-". This will fill the cell with a row of minus signs. Now do the same in B10. Move to B12 and this time enter "\=", to fill the cell with equality signs.

Go to B1 (the title) and press F2 to edit the contents of the cell. Move to the beginning of the line and delete the single quote mark there. The fastest way to do this is by pressing Home and then Delete. Making sure that the program is in Insert mode (look at the bottom line of the display, to see if Overwrite is displayed there), add a "^" to the beginning of the line. The line should now appear as "^Car Expenses". Repeat this procedure at B2.

Remembering the design tips given in 4.4, enter labels of ">This line centred" into C1 and C2. The greater than sign (>) means nothing as part of the label and is used merely to point to the note.

4.9 Changing column widths

Occasionally, the width of a column may be too small to allow numbers and text to be displayed properly. If a number is too large to be shown, it will be represented on the screen by a line of asterisks. The following procedure allows you to change the width of any column. A change that affects only part of a worksheet is said to act LOCALLY.

* Press "/" to access the main menu.

* Select "Worksheet" (the first menu entry).

* From the Worksheet sub-menu, select "ColWidth" (Column Width).

* From the Column Width sub-menu, select "Set".

* Type in the new width for the column and press Enter. You can also use the cursor keys to shrink or expand the width of the column before pressing Enter.

The abbreviation for this command is "/WCS".

The default column width is nine characters. To change the default setting, use the procedure that follows. Note that the default settings only apply to those columns that have not been changed manually. A change such as this, that effects the whole of the worksheet, is said to act GLOBALLY.

* Press "/" to access the main menu.

* Select "Worksheet" (the first menu entry).

* From the Worksheet sub-menu, select "General".

* From the General sub-menu, select "Column".

* Type in a new default width and press Enter. You can also use the cursor keys to shrink or expand the width of the column before pressing Enter.

The abbreviation for this command is "/WGC".

4.10 Marking a range of cells.

Some commands can be used on a single cell or can be applied to a block of cells at the same time. Blocks of cells can be marked or highlighted in two ways.

* Type the co-ordinate of the first cell (top left corner of the block) followed by two full stops and the co-ordinate of the last cell (bottom right corner of the block). Thus, to mark all of the cells in the block A1 to E20, you would type "A1..E20".

* Move to the top left corner of the block you wish to mark and press the full stop key (.). If the marking operation has already begun, you may need to press Escape to "free" the cursor. When the "." key is pressed, it "anchors" the cursor to the current cell. As you move around the worksheet, you will see that all of the cells contained between the "anchor" and the current cursor position are highlighted. Move to the bottom right corner of the block, making sure that all of the cells you want to mark are highlighted, and press Enter.

If you wish to apply an operation to only the current cell, ignore the block marking function and simply press Enter twice. This sets the size of the block to the current cell location. For example, pressing Enter twice at A1 would be the same as typing "A1..A1".

You can step backwards through a marking operation by using the Escape key.

A range of cells can also be given a name, so that various commands can be made to operate on the entire range. The "Name" command is used as follows:

* Access the main menu by pressing the "/" key.

* Select "Range" from the main menu.

* Select "Name" from the Range sub-menu

* Select "Create" from the Name sub-menu

* Enter a meaningful name for the range, remembering that the maximum length for a name is 11 characters

* Highlight the range of cells you wish to apply the name to using one of the methods described earlier

Additionally, the following commands can also be used when working with named ranges:

* A single range name can be deleted by repeating the above process, substituting "Delete" for "Create".

* All of the range names in the current worksheet can be deleted by selecting "Reset" from the Name sub-menu.

* A table of all current range names can be inserted into the worksheet by using the "Table" command from the Name sub-menu. Note that the cursor should be located in an empty section of the worksheet before invoking the command.

4.11 Formatting a range of cells.

All spreadsheets have the ability to display the contents of cells in a variety of ways. This is done by FORMATTING a range of cells. The formats available are:

* Fixed. Numbers are displayed with to a fixed number of decimal places. For example, 123.45

* Scientific. Numbers are shown in scientific notation, using three decimals. For example, 123.456E+8

* Comma. Numbers are displayed with thousands are separated by commas. For example, 1,234,567

* Currency. Numbers are displayed with two decimal places and are preceded by a currency symbol (which can be changed). For example, £123.45

* Percent. Numbers are shown as percentages, with no decimal places. For example, 45%

* General. This is the default format for cells and appears to display values with a greater accuracy than the other formats (since more decimal places are used). However, this is misleading since all values are calculated with the same degree of accuracy.

* Text. Displays the formulas contained in cells, as opposed to the results of the calculations.

* +/-. Values are represented as being negative or positive. For example, +++++

* Date. Sets how the date and time are to be displayed.

* Hide. Hides the contents of a cell.

* Reset. Resets the format of a cell back to the General format.

To change the format of a cell or range of cells, carry out the steps that follow. The procedure can be abbreviated to "/RF".

* Access the main menu by pressing the "/" key.

* Select "Range" from the main menu.

* From the Range sub-menu, select "Format".

* From the Format sub-menu choose the format you wish to apply to the range.

* Some options require you to specify further information, such as the number of decimal places to display. If a menu is presented, select the option you want from it. Otherwise, type in the required data and press Enter.

* Mark the range of cells to apply the formatting command to (see 4.10) and press Enter.

4.12 Improving the presentation of the worksheet (3).

As mentioned before, some of the information contained in the column B of the worksheet "overflows" into column C. To remedy this, change the column width (see 4.9) of B to 16 by using the following steps:

* Press "/" to access the main menu.

* From the main menu, select "Worksheet".

* From the Worksheet sub-menu, select "Column"

* From the Column sub-menu, select "Set"

* Type "16" and press Enter.

As usual, this can be abbreviated to: "/WCS followed by 16". Having changed the column width, you should now see that the title line has become centred. Now, let's enter a note in B14 to remind ourselves and other users that the column has been changed. Move to B14 and enter "Column width changed to 16" as a label.

Since we are dealing with sums of money, we should change the format of the numbers in cells B4..B9 and B11 to currency.

* Press "/" to access the main menu.

* Select "Range" from the main menu.

* From the Range sub-menu, select "Format".

* From the Format sub-menu, select "Currency".

* If we were only concerned with whole pounds or dollars, we would enter zero as the number of decimal places to display. However, in this case, two decimal places are fine, so just press Enter to accept the default value.

* Move to B4 and press the "." key. This causes the cell to become an "anchor", fixing the position of the top left-hand corner of the block to be formatted.

* Move to B9 (the bottom right-hand corner of the block to be formatted) and press Enter. The format of all of the cells from B4 to B9 should change instantaneously to show all of the values in the range as currency.

This can be abbreviated to "/RFC". Move to B11 and repeat the entire process except that this time, there is no need to define a range of cells to be formatted. Instead, accept the default start co-ordinate of B11 by pressing Enter, and then fix the end co-ordinate to B11 also by pressing Enter again.

Note that cell formatting is non-destructive in nature. If a cell contains a value when it is formatted, that value will not be erased. Similarly, a cell need not contain a value to be formatted, but when one is entered, it will be displayed in the current format. This will be demonstrated in a little while, when the final car expenses total is calculated. You should also note that formats applied to labels are harmless and do not change the way in which the label is displayed.

Go to C4 and enter a label of ">Formatted as currency".

We are now going to cause cell B11 to calculate the total of the values stored in B4..B9. Move to B11 and enter the following: "@SUM(B4..B9)".

The "@" symbol precedes a built-in formula, followed by a key word. In this case, they key word "SUM" adds together all of the values in a specified block. The final part of the formula specifies the range of cells that the command should encompass. You can see that the range is specified in the same way as described in 4.10. Breaking the formula down then, we have "add together all of the values contained in the cells from B4 to B9". Once more, the worksheet is updated almost instantaneously and the correct total is displayed as currency.

Finally, go to C11 and enter a label of "> Contains formula @SUM(B4..B9)".

This completes the sample worksheet, which should now appear as shown below.

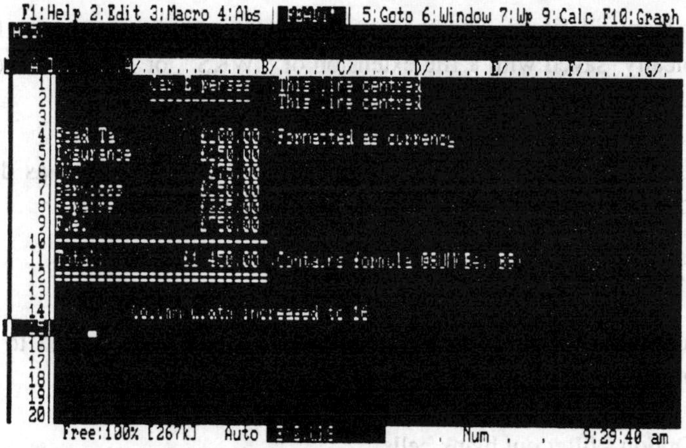

Try changing some or all of the values in cells B4 to B9. As you do this, notice that any changes you make cause the total in B11 to be updated almost instantly. Try entering some negative numbers (just use a minus sign to precede the number) to see how they affect the cell's display and the total calculation. Before making any changes, make a note of the original numbers in each cell, so you can replace them later on.

4.13 Saving and loading worksheets

The File menu offers the following options:

* Retrieve - load a file from disk.

* Store - save a file to disk.

* Xport - save the contents of a range of cells to disk as a worksheet or a dBase III file.

* Import - load a file from disk, interpreting values, text or dBase III data. If "values" is chosen, the program translates the import file into values and formulas. Translating a file in this way is known as PARSING. If "text" is chosen, the program treats the data in the import file as labels.

* Erase - delete a file from disk. A sub-menu allows user to select from only those files containing a "W" or "P" as the first letter of the extension

or from all files. The reason for this is that spreadsheet files are typically saved with a file extension of ".WKS" or "WK1" and report data is normally saved in files with the extension ".PRT".

* List - list the files in the current directory. A sub-menu as described above allows different kinds of files to be viewed.

* Dir - set the data directory to use.

* Uplink - update the data contained in any cells linked to another worksheet.

* Option - filter out blank cells.

To save a file, you must first decide which directory or sub directory you wish to use. If this is not the same as the current directory, it must be changed using the "Dir" option. If you are unsure about paths and file specifications, refer to your MS-DOS manual for more information. As an example, let's assume we want to change from "D:\ASEASYAS" to "C:\ WKSHEET".

* Access the main menu with the "/" key.

* Select "File" from the main menu.

* From the File sub-menu, select "Dir". The current path will appear at the top of the screen.

* The cursor position is at the beginning of the line. If you want to edit the line, use the arrow keys to move along it and make any changes you need. Otherwise, pressing any letter key will delete the entire line so that you can type in all of the new path manually. Since we wish to change to another drive, start to type "C:\WKSHEET". As soon as the first letter is pressed, the old line is deleted and the new line begins to appear. Press Enter when you have finished.

Next, you must choose a file name for the worksheet. The name should be meaningful, so that you will still be able to remember what the file contains in a few months' time. File names can contain eight characters and the extension should always be ".WKS" or ".WK1", depending on which program you are using. If you are unsure about choosing a valid file name, refer to your MS-DOS manual for more information.

If you are already in the File menu, choose "Store", otherwise use "/F" before choosing "Store".

You are now prompted to type in the file name. If the file was previously loaded from disk, the correct name will already be displayed. In this case, just press Enter to save it back to disk under the same name. For new files, type in a suitable file name and press Enter.

If you want to check whether or not a file name already exists, use the "List" option from the File sub- menu and choose "W??" to show all of the worksheet files in the current directory.

To load a file, move into the File sub-menu and choose "Retrieve". A list of worksheet files will appear on the screen and you can highlight the file you want to load by using the cursor keys. Press Enter when the correct file name is highlighted and the worksheet will load automatically.

You will notice that ":\" often appears in the corner of the directory window. Selecting this allows you to move up and down through the directory structure of the current drive. Sub directories are shown with a "\" preceding them. Positioning the cursor on a sub directory and pressing Enter moves you into that sub directory. Selecting ":\" moves you back up one level in the directory structure. In this way, you can search the entire contents of a disk drive to locate worksheet files.

4.14 Saving the sample worksheet

The final part of this exercise involves some copying and moving operations that should be carried out only after the worksheet has been saved.

To save the sample worksheet, do the following:

* Press "/" to access the main menu.

* From the main menu, select "File".

* From the File menu, choose "Store".

* Type "EX1_CAR.WKS" as the file name to store the worksheet under. In file names, the underscore character is often used instead of a space. The character is obtained by holding the Shift key down and pressing the minus button. The file name chosen should be easy to remember in the future because "EX1" stands for "Exercise 1" and the word "Car" reminds you that the worksheet is to do with motoring expenses. Press Enter to save the file to disk.

The abbreviated commands for accessing the File menu are: "/F". To store a file, the abbreviated command would be "/FS" followed by the file name and Enter.

We will be loading the sample worksheet back into the program after the copying operation, so here are the instructions for doing this:

* Press "/" to access the main menu.

* From the main menu, select "File".

* From the File menu, choose "Retrieve".

* Move the cursor with the arrow keys until "EX1_CAR.WKS" is highlighted. Press Enter to load the file.

The abbreviated commands for loading a file are: "/FR".

4.15 Copying cells

The Copy command allows you to make exact copies of the data contained in a range of cells. Copying requires a SOURCE (where you copy from) and a DESTINATION (where you copy to) and is a block command. When a cell is copied to another location, the destination cell will have the same format as the source. If a formula is copied to another location, any cell co-ordinates it contains will be altered to become relative to the formula's new position.

To copy a block of cells:

* Move to the top left-hand corner of the block you want to copy.

* Select "Copy".

* Access the main menu by pressing the "/" key.

* Move to the bottom right-hand corner of the block you want to copy and press Enter.

* Move to the top left-hand corner of the area you want to copy the block into and press Enter.

The Copy command is extremely versatile since it is based on blocks rather than single cells. In other words, this command lets you copy a single cell or block to just one location or a whole block of locations. This can be demonstrated by the following set of commands.

To make multiple copies of a single cell:

* Move to the cell you want to copy.

* Access the main menu by pressing the "/" key.

* Select "Copy".

* Press Enter to make the program treat the cell as a block.

* Move to the top left-hand corner of the block you want to fill with copies and press ".".

* Move to the bottom right-hand corner of the block you want to fill with copies and press Enter.

The procedure is essentially the same if you want to make multiple copies of a block. The difference is that instead of marking a single cell as the source a whole block is marked instead.

The abbreviation for a copying procedure is "/C".

Cell references (co-ordinates), such as those used in formulas, can be fixed or variable. Unless otherwise specified, the default for cell references is that they are variable, that is, when cells are copied or moved, each reference is altered so that it remains correct. This is known as a RELATIVE co-ordinate. A fixed cell reference, one that retains the same value regardless of changes made to the worksheet, is called an ABSOLUTE co-ordinate. Copying operations do not alter absolute references.

4.16 Moving cells

The Move command operates in a similar way to the Copy command. In a Move operation, the source cells are copied to the destination area of the worksheet and the original is then erased. As with the Copy command, formulas are changed so that they are relevant to the moved cells' new position but formatting is not retained.

To move a single cell or a range of cells:

* Move to the top left-hand corner of the block you want to move.

* Press the "/" key to access the main menu.

* Select "Move".

* If only want to move one cell, press Enter to make the program treat the cell as a block. Otherwise, move to the bottom right-hand corner of the source block and press Enter.

* Move to the top left-hand corner of the area you want to move the block into and press Enter.

The abbreviation for a Move operation is "/M". Note that Move does not affect absolute references (see above).

4.17 Copying and moving cells in the sample worksheet

These last few operations with the sample worksheet will give you some practical experience in copying and moving cells. As you carry these procedures out, notice what happens to the format of cells and how the formula changes to reflect its new position in the worksheet.

* Go to B4 and press "C" from the main menu (/) to choose "Copy".

* Highlight the range B4 to B11.

* Move to C4 and press Enter to copy the marked block.

If you are not sure what to do, look further back in this section for information on how to highlight and copy cells.

Next, change the column width to 16, so that all of the numbers and results of the formula can be viewed properly. The illustration shows how the worksheet should have changed. The labels we entered previously into the C column have been overwritten by the new information. All of the copied cells have retained their formats and the formula has changed to "@SUM(C4..C9)". Notice that the total is still correct and that the formula now relates to the values in C4 to C9.

You can experiment further by copying cells to other locations. Try copying the B4..B11 range across a number of columns and see what happens. You should find that multiple copies of the range have been made and that each copy of the formula relates to the column it is in.

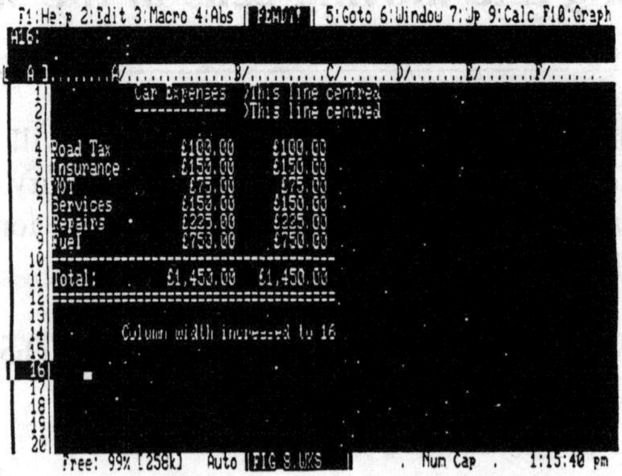

Load the original worksheet, "EX1_CAR.WKS", back into the program (see 4.14) and try moving some cells as follows.

* Go to B4 and press "M" from the main menu (/) to choose "Move".

* Highlight the range B4 to B11.

* Move to C4 and press Enter to move the marked block.

This time, the cells are copied into their new location and the "original" column is deleted. Once again, the formula has changed to reflect its new position and the total remains accurate. Although the format of the cells has been retained, you'll see that the column width is still set to the default value. To

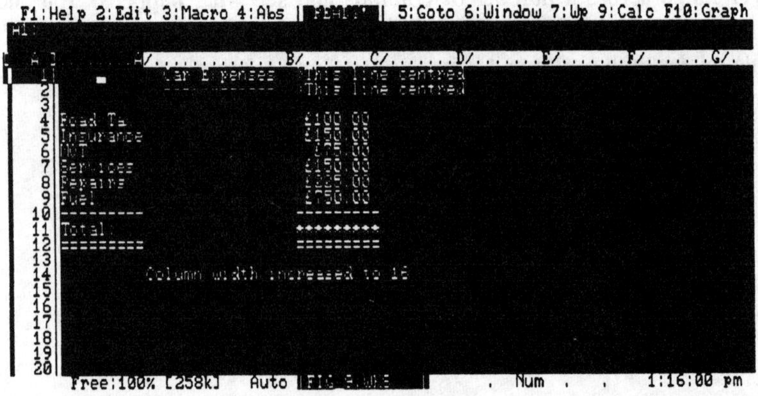

view the total properly, change the column width to 12 with the sequence "/WCS".

Feel free to experiment by changing values in the worksheet or adding new labels. Read the next sections on hiding cells and inserting/deleting cells before continuing. See how these functions might be used to improve the presentation of your worksheet by hiding potentially confusing formulas or making space to add helpful comments. If the worksheet becomes messy, remember that the original is stored safely on disk and can be recalled at any time.

Incidentally, this worksheet will not be used again, so it can be erased from the disk, if you wish.

4.18 Inserting and deleting rows or columns

As you begin to construct a worksheet, you occasionally find that it is necessary to insert new rows or columns, for example to create a space that can be used to add comments. The procedure for inserting new rows and columns is as follows:

* Press "/" to access the main menu

* Select "W" to access the Worksheet sub-menu

* Select "I" to access the Insert sub-menu

* Select "R" for rows or "C" for columns

* Press Enter to insert a new row or column at the cursor position.

Remember that the new row or column is inserted before the cursor position. For example, if you wanted to insert a new column between A1 and B1, you would move the cursor to B1 before using the Insert command.

The keystroke sequences for these operations are "/WIC" or "/WIR".

You can insert more than one row or column at a time by "anchoring" the cursor in the current cell and then using the cursor keys to move a number of positions down or across before pressing Enter. For example, to insert 4 new columns between A1 and B1:

Move the cursor to the insertion point (B1) using the cursor keys

Use the command sequence "/WIC"

Press the "." key to anchor the cursor at the insertion point (B1)

Press the right arrow 4 times. The number of columns that will be inserted will be highlighted.

Press Enter to insert the columns

Rows and columns can be deleted in almost the same way. This is done by selecting "Delete" instead of "Insert" from the Worksheet sub-menu. Again, more than one row or column can be deleted at a time by highlighting a range of cells using the "." key. Remember that errors will be generated if any of the formulas or cell references that remain point to cells that have been deleted.

4.19 Hiding sections of a worksheet

It is a good idea to hide any section of a worksheet that might cause confusion to a user. This technique can also be used to improve the overall presentation of the worksheet, so that it appears clear, concise and well structured.

The "Hide" command effectively reduces the width of a cell displayed on the screen to zero, rendering it invisible. Note that only the way in which the cell is displayed is altered; the contents remain unchanged and the accuracy of any value stored in the cell is not affected.

Cells can be hidden as follows:

* Press "/" to access the main menu

* Press "R" to access the Range sub-menu

* From the Range menu, press "F" to call the Format sub-menu

* Select "Hide" as the format to apply to the cells you wish to alter

* Highlight the range of cells you wish to hide in the normal way (see 4.10) and press Enter

All of the cells hidden in this way can be returned to their original display format by repeating the process above, using "Reset" instead of "Hide" as the formatting command.

4.20 Summary

In this section, you have learned how to:

* Erase a worksheet from memory

* Align text

* Fill cells with repetitions of the same character

* Define ranges of cells

* Format ranges of cells

* Enter a formula

* Copy cells

* Move cells

* Change the width of a column

* Insert and delete rows and columns

* "Hide" sections of a worksheet

* Save and restore worksheets from disk

Section 5: Simple Models

5.1 Objective

This exercise is designed to show how spreadsheet models can be applied to a wide variety of common applications. Unlike other tutorials, the emphasis of this section is on the practical skills needed to construct models for "real life" situations. In this case, the exercise concerns a simple cash flow forecast for a fictional company. The skills and concepts introduced during the course of the exercise are not limited to cash flow forecasts: they can also be applied to areas as diverse as keeping track of a personal bank account or creating budgets for household bills. Upon completion of the cash flow exercise, an average reader should be capable of producing worksheets capable of handling the majority of their needs.

5.2 Designing a worksheet.

The layout of a large application needs to be planned very carefully in advance. At a basic level, perhaps the easiest way of doing this is to divide a sheet of paper into a number of squares and then mark out where each area of the worksheet will appear. Since worksheets can be extremely large, the exact co- ordinates of each area are largely irrelevant. However, it is common for people to use grid sizes of 26 cells across and 50 cells deep. This gives work areas with boundary co-ordinates that are easy to remember. The diagram below shows how this can be done.

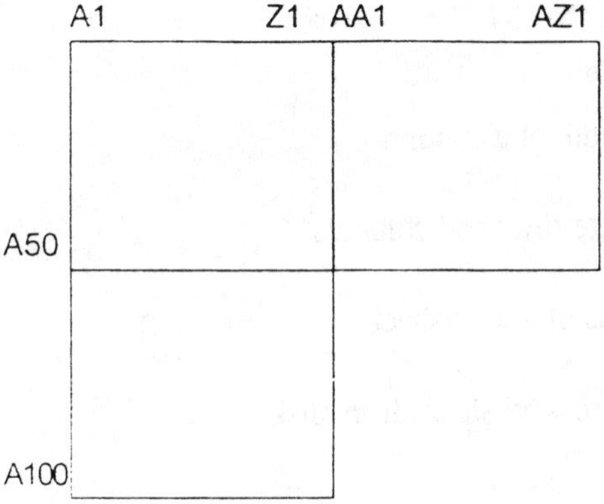

A good preliminary design:

* Simplifies the structure of the worksheet

* Reduces overall development time

* Reduces the number of errors that can be made when constructing the worksheet

* Improves presentation

* Allows enhancements and amendments to be made more easily

The kind of approach described above forms the basis of a development routine that allows each section of the worksheet to be created in near isolation. Once an item has been tested and is deemed satisfactory, it can then be integrated into the whole. With a little care, this modular approach also allows users to create a library of useful routines that can be "bolted on" to future worksheets. Not only does this reduce development time, but it also brings a sense of uniformity to worksheets created by the same company or individual.

It is already possible to buy entire sets of ready-made worksheets, prepared so that only the customer's own data needs to be entered for the application to be complete. These worksheets are known as TEMPLATES and are available from a variety of sources including Public Domain libraries. Users can create their own templates in the same way.

At a more advanced level, the development process becomes similar to a systems analysis approach; requirements are analysed, resources (the facilities of the spreadsheet program, existing templates etc.) are identified and a detailed specification is drawn up before any work begins with the software itself. With a good working knowledge of the spreadsheet program and experience of software design, any user should be able to create a diagrammatic design system tailored to their specific needs.

5.3 The design of the cash flow forecast worksheet

Here is a simple diagram of the overall layout of the cash flow forecast worksheet that will be created during the next exercise:

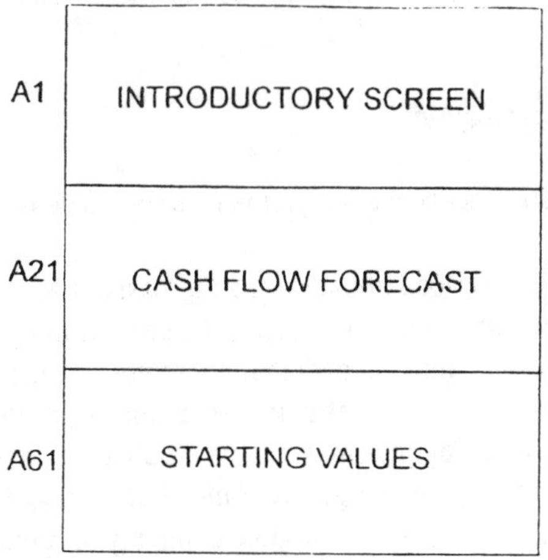

The "top down" design is deliberate, although the intention is not to draw a parallel between worksheet design and program development. In the next exercise, the layout of the cash flow forecast will be changed dramatically, to allow for the introduction of a range of new features.

5.4 Using introductory screens.

An introductory screen is an important feature of any large model. The list below summarises the information that the introduction should provide for users. The importance of each item should be apparent without any further explanation.

* The title of the worksheet, including the company's name (if any)

* The purpose of the worksheet

* The name and designation of the person who constructed the worksheet

* Important instructions to users

* The location of each different section of the model

* Macro key assignments

* Maintenance information, such as the date of the last modification

5.5 Setting starting values.

There are two common errors that users make when constructing large worksheets. The first is to use a set of values (as opposed to formulas) in the "body" of the worksheet. Often, these values are copied directly into other areas of the worksheet, causing it to become unwieldy and awkward to modify. When a change needs to be implemented, this approach means that each and every occurrence of the data must be edited manually.

The second common error is making multiple copies of data in an attempt to make the development process a little easier. If a relationship has not been established between each copy of the data, the accuracy of the model becomes threatened. For example, one might change the contents of one copy of a cell without posting the amendment to every other copy. Additionally, this approach means that the appearance of the worksheet is spoiled and the overall structure becomes too complicated to allow for easy maintenance.

A side-effect of developing worksheets in this way is that the ability of the model to carry out "what if?" calculations become severely restricted.

It is a good idea to group together all of the variable information that will be used in the worksheet. In simple terms, this means having only point of origin for each value that is used in the application. You can still copy the information to other areas of the worksheet by using a simple formula. This way, any change that is made to the original value will be carried over to each copy.

A good example would be a worksheet designed to calculate the overall cost of producing a single item. Imagine if a set of fixed material, labour and power costs were copied to perhaps a dozen separate areas of the worksheet. If any of these costs changed, the user would need to work through every single area of the worksheet and change the figures manually. However, if every area of the worksheet read each cost from a single location, only one cell would need to be changed to affect the entire worksheet. This way, it would also take just a few seconds to see what the effects of, say, a sudden increase in the labour charge would be.

The benefits of creating a set of starting values for a worksheet can be summarised as follows:

* The risk of introducing errors into the worksheet is reduced

* Presentation is improved

* Maintenance is made easier

* The use of formulas to access each value means that "What if?" calculations become possible

* Additional features, such as data entry screens, can be added to the model more easily

If this still seems a little unclear, see the next section on creating a set of starting values for the cash flow forecast used in the exercise.

5.6 Preparing to create the cash flow forecast.

The cash flow forecast used in this exercise is intentionally crude since the next exercises build upon this elementary worksheet to create a more complex model. In this worksheet, we are concerned only with:

* A clumsy estimate of monthly sales growth

* The basic costs of producing an item

* The monthly cost of the company's premises

* Monthly income from a small investment

However, one of the design briefs given is that the worksheet must be capable of showing the effects of any changes to the above factors. With this in mind, which values should be capable of being modified?

It is fair to say that the selling price will be increased at least once a year. Similarly, we can expect to see increases in the costs of materials, labour, power and rental of premises. The small investment mentioned earlier might also experience some changes, particularly if a proportion of the company's annual profits is added to the lump sum each year. Finally, we will assume that the company is working with a new product that has a growing demand; a "rising star".

Although the name of the company and the type of product are unimportant in this model, we will keep with traditional accounting exercises and call the product a "widget". Since the company is relatively new and aims to dominate the world widget market, we will call it "MegaWidget International".

Let's assign some arbitrary values to the variable factors that have just been identified.

Selling Price: £9.55
Current level of sales: 1000 units per month
Expected sales growth: 5% per month
Cost of materials per unit: £5.75
Labour cost per unit: £1.23
Cost of power per unit: £0.77
Premises: £3000 per month
Amount of investment: £25000
Annual interest rate: 12%

To make things as simple as possible, we will go a little further and make three basic assumptions. The first is that all costs are dealt with in the month they are incurred. The second is that all incoming payments are received in the same month that the goods are delivered. Finally, the company's banking arrangements include no charges for negative balances, meaning that overdraft facilities are completely free of charge.

5.7 Entering calculations into a worksheet

You should not feel daunted by the apparent complexity of the calculations you will encounter in a worksheet. Very simply, if you can evaluate a formula using a scientific calculator, you can use mathematics in a spreadsheet.

Spreadsheet calculations can refer to the contents of a cell or work directly on numbers. Calculations can be divided into formulas and functions.

FORMULAS are mathematical expressions, similar to the calculations you would make using a pocket calculator. For example, the formula "+5+7-2" would return a value of "10". Although it is not always necessary, it is a good idea to enclose all formulas in brackets. This reduces the possibility of mistaking a formula for a value when glancing quickly through a worksheet. For example, it would be quite easy to mistake "7" for "+7" or vice versa.

FUNCTIONS use the spreadsheet's built-in facilities and are preceded by the "@" symbol. For example, "@ABS(-7)" would return the absolute value of the expression, in this case, "7". Functions must always be entered according to a specific format (SYNTAX). The syntax for a function is usually in the form of:

```
@Function Name(Argument 1, Argument 2...)
```

Arguments can include values, cell references, formulas or other functions.

To enter a function or formula:

* Move the cell which will be used to store the function or formula

* Type the function or formula just as you would a number; without a label prefix (see 4.6) and using the correct syntax. Press Enter when finished.

5.8 Adding the initial values to the sample worksheet.

The "initial values" section of the worksheet employs some important techniques that will be relevant to most applications:

* The section begins with a title that gives a clear description of the purpose of the section

* Each value is labelled clearly and indicates how long the quantity refers to; per month, per annum etc.

* Each value is followed by a unit of measurement; pounds, units, per cent etc.

* In order to simplify the calculations that will be used in the cash flow forecast area of the worksheet, some values have been pre-calculated. For example, the annual interest rate for the investment has been converted to a monthly figure. Although the diagram does not show the whole of this section, these calculated values are also clearly labelled.

If you look at the illustration closely, you will see that percentage figures have been divided by 100, so that later calculations can be simplified. Normally, calculating the monthly effect on a figure of an annual growth of, say, 5% would involve a calculation such as:

```
(X+(X*((5/12)/100)))
```

Assuming that X is the value we are working with, this could be broken down into a series of steps:

* Divide the annual rate of growth by 12 to give a monthly rate of growth

* Divide the monthly rate of growth by 100 to give a fraction expressed as a decimal

* Multiply X by the decimal to give the growth for one month

* Add X to the figure for the monthly growth to give the final answer

An easier way of doing this is to calculate monthly growth in advance and store the result in a cell. In the example above, this could be done with this calculation:

```
((5/12)/100)
```

Let's assume that the result of the calculation above is stored in A1. To calculate the monthly growth, we just add 1 to the value in A1 and multiply this by X. The calculation in the worksheet could then be expressed as:

```
(X*(1+A1))
```

This is clearly far simpler than the calculation we began with and gives two important advantages. Firstly, since the calculation is broken down into a series of steps, it is easier to implement. Secondly, a great deal of needless repetition is avoided, making the worksheet easier to follow and reducing the number of calculations that need to be made by the program.

You can see how this has been done in the sample worksheet at co-ordinates E65 and E72.

Enter the information given in 5.6 so that it appears as shown in the diagram below. Note as the worksheet progresses that each area is located so that users can reach it as easily as possible. For example, this section begins at A61 - reached from the Home position (A1) by pressing the Page Down key three times.

The list that follows describes the data that should be entered into each cell. Cell co-ordinates are shown in the brackets and labels are enclosed in quotes. Each line shows how the row will read across.

```
(A61) "Starting Values For MegaWidget Cash flow Forecast"
(A63) "Selling Price", (C63) 9.55, (D63) "£"
(A64) "Starting Sales", (C64) 1000, (D64) "units"
(A65) "Sales Growth P.M.", (C65) 5, (D65) "% Giving"
(A66) "Materials Cost P.U.", (C66) 5.75, (D66) "£"
(A67) "Labour Cost P.U.", (C67) 1.23, (D67) "£"
(A68) "Power Cost P.U.", (C68) 0.77, (D68) "£"
(A69) "Monthly Rental", (C69) 3000, (D69) "£"
(A70) "Savings Account", (C70) 25000, (D70) "£"
(A71) "Interest Rate P.A.", (C71) 12, (D71) "% - Or", (F71) "%
Per Month"
(D72) "- Giving"
```

Additionally, enter the following formulas:

```
At E65 enter  "@(C65/100)"
At E71 enter "@(C71/12)"
At E72 enter "@(E71/100)"
```

These formulas produce the figures by which monthly sales growth and savings account interest will be calculated later on. Note the use of relative co-ordinates in each of these formulas, which ensure that any changes made to the starting values in C71 and C65 will be accounted for automatically.

Remember that all of this data is entered by simply moving to the correct location in the worksheet, typing the entry and then pressing Enter.

As a final touch, to make this section a little more presentable, alter the column width from the default value of 9 to 16.

* From the main menu, select "Worksheet"

* Now select "ColWidth"

* Select "Set" from the Column Width sub-menu and enter a new value of 16.

The abbreviation for this set of commands is "/WCS".

By design, this new value will also improve the appearance of labels entered into the cash flow area a little later on.

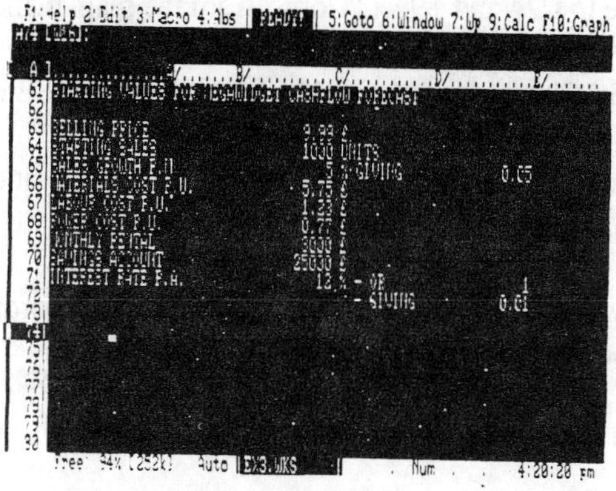

5.9 Building the sample cash flow forecast

Having established a series of initial values, we can now start to build the cash flow forecast. The first part of the operation involves the rather tedious process of entering labels. However, this is an excellent opportunity for you to reinforce the basic skills learned in earlier sections.

I. Move to A21 and enter a title of "MegaWidget International - Cash flow Forecast". You will recall that titles should include a description of the purpose of the worksheet or section and the company name.

II. Next, work across from C23 to N23 and enter the names of the months. Centre the label text by preceding each name with the "^" character. Thus, in C23 you would enter "^JAN", in D23 you would enter "^FEB" and so on.

III. At C24, fill the cell with equality signs by entering the "repeat" character, followed by an equality sign (see 4.7); "\=".

IV. Copy C24 to the range D24..N24 (see 4.15). To do this:

* Move to C24 and select "Copy" from the main menu.

* Mark C24 as the source block by pressing the Enter key once.

* Move to D24 and anchor the cursor at this position by pressing the "." key.

* Move to N24 and press Enter to mark this co-ordinate as the end of the block to copy to, completing the operation.

The abbreviation for a Copy command is "/C".

V. Enter "Subtotal" as a label at P23, using the "^" character to centre it, giving an entry of "^Subtotal".

VI. Copy any one cell from the range C24..N24 to P24, effectively underlining the label you have just entered. This is exactly the same as copying a cell to a block, except that there is no need to anchor the cursor since P24 is both the start and end co-ordinate of the block:

* Move to C24 and select "Copy" from the main menu.

* Mark C24 as the source block by pressing the Enter key once.

* Move to P24 and press Enter to mark this co-ordinate as both the start and the end of the block to copy to.

The same series of commands would work equally well with any cell in the range C24..N24 since the contents are identical. Thus, in the instructions above, C24 could be replaced by any of D24, E24... and so on.

VII. At A25, enter a label of "Cash Inflows". Fill A26 with minus signs by entering "\-".

VIII. Working downwards, enter labels of "Sales (Units)", "Sales (£)" and "Interest" in positions A27, A28 and A29 respectively.

IX. Enter a label of "Subtotal" in A31. Fill A30 and A31 with minus signs ("\-").

X. Enter a label of "Cash Outflows" at A34. Fill A35 with a row of minus signs ("\-"). Working downwards, enter labels of "Materials", "Labour", "Power, Light, Heat" and "Premises" in cells A36, A37, A38 and A39 respectively.

XI. Enter a label of "Subtotal" in A41. Fill both A40 and A42 with a row of minus signs ("\-").

XII. In A45 enter a label of "Monthly Balance". Fill both A44 and A46 with a row of equality signs ("\=").

XIII. Copy the cells at positions A30, A32, A40, A42, A44 and A46 across the row so that end under the "DEC" label, in the N column.

* Position the cursor on the first cell (for example, A30). Select "Copy" from the main menu.

* Press Enter to mark the current cell as the source block.

* Move to the next cell horizontally (for example, B30). Press the "." key to mark this as the start of the block to copy to.

* Move to the N column (for example, N30) and press Enter to mark this as the end of the block to copy to.

So that we can see the contents of worksheet properly, we will need to change the width of each column from B to P. Eventually, we will also need to format these columns to display information as currency.

We can estimate what the new column width should be by considering a number of factors. Firstly, if values are displayed to two decimal places, three characters will be used for the decimal (.XX). Secondly, negative values will be enclosed in brackets giving us a further two characters to account for. Finally, it is unlikely - in the case of MegaWidget International - that we will be dealing with amounts in excess of £1000,000, meaning that we need only reserve 58characters in order to be able to cope with sums of up to £999,999.

Thus, we can estimate the new width of the column by examining how many characters are required to display the largest possible value we wish to deal with. For MegaWidget International, this would be a negative value of £999,999.99 and would be shown as: (£999,999.99). The total number of characters required to display this value is 13.

Change the width of each column from B to P to a new value of 13 by repeating the following in each column:

* Move to any cell in the column you wish to change

* Select "Worksheet" from the main menu.

* Select "ColWidth" from the Worksheet sub-menu.

* Select "Set" from the Column Width sub-menu

* Type 13 and press Enter

The abbreviation for this set of commands is: "/WCS".

Although incomplete, the worksheet should now appear in the format shown below.

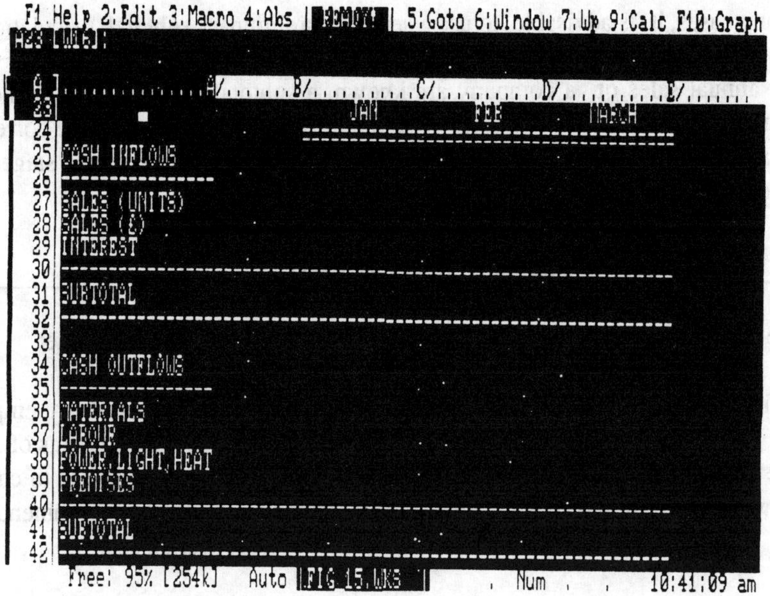

5.10 Order of work

In order to test the accuracy of the worksheet as work progresses and to reduce the risk of errors, a methodical approach must be taken.

In most cases, breaking the worksheet down into separate sections, as described in section 5.2, allows work to be carried out in each section in the order of left to right and top to bottom.

Each subsection of the worksheet can be broken down further by attempting to enter calculations following the scheme of:

* Detail lines

* Subtotals

* Totals

In many cases, it is advisable to use a series of preliminary subtotal calculations so that the accuracy of each set of detail lines can be tested. For example, if the total annual sales of a company are known, a subtotal calculation will show whether or not the figures relating to a monthly sales breakdown are correct. This approach allows the accuracy of the model to be tested at each stage of development.

5.11 Copying values into a cell

There are two basic methods of copying a value from one cell to another.

The first is to use an addition sign to add the value to the contents of an empty cell. For example, "+A1" is a simple formula that means "add the contents of A1 to the current cell". Since the current cell is empty, the net effect is to copy over whatever is stored in A1. However, this method is not to be recommended since it might cause confusion when working with large worksheets.

The second is to enclose the cell co-ordinate in brackets, for example "(A1)". This method is to be preferred since it is simple and unambiguous.

Note that these methods do not copy formulas - only the results of them. To copy the contents of a cell in its entirety, the "Copy" command (see 4.15) must be used.

5.12 Fixing absolute co-ordinates in a calculation

See section 4.15 for an explanation of *absolute* and *relative* co-ordinates.

Imagine copying a formula of "(+A1)" from A2 to B2. Since the co-ordinate given is relative, the copy of the formula will appear as "(+B1)". The program has altered the co-ordinate so that it is RELATIVE to the position of the copied cell in the worksheet.

This can be avoided by specifying that the co-ordinate - or just part of it - is to be treated as an ABSOLUTE location. The way that is done is by inserting a dollar sign ($) before each part of the co-ordinate. There are three possible ways to use the "$" symbol:

$A1 - the column reference will remain fixed but the row reference will alter. For example, A1 might become A2 or A3.

A$1 - the row reference will remain fixed but the column reference will alter. For example, A1 might become B1 or C1.

$A$1 - both parts of the co-ordinate are fixed and will not alter.

5.13 Calculating the Cash Inflows.

Now that the skeleton of the worksheet has been created, it is time to enter the formulas and functions that will complete the cash flow forecast. The design of the cash flow area divides the section neatly into three main areas:

* Cash Inflows

* Cash Outflows

* Totals

Beginning with the "Cash Inflows" area, we will start by working across the "Sales (Units)" row. The figure for starting sales in January was established when we entered all of the starting values for the worksheet. As you will recall, starting sales were 1000 units per month. This means that January's sales figure can be copied directly from the initial value located at C64. This can be done by entering "(C64)" into C27 (January's sales in units).

In February, sales have grown by a fraction and this must be accounted for in the calculation. The growth rate (5%) is given in the starting values area of the worksheet, at co-ordinate C65. Additionally, you should recall that we took the opportunity to convert the growth rate into a decimal fraction that simplified the growth calculation. This value is stored in E65. Thus, the figure for February's sales is obtained by multiplying January's sales by 1 plus the value in E65. This gives us a formula of (C27*(1+E65)) to be placed in D27.

The same calculation will be used for the remainder of the year. For example, the sales figure for March is obtained by multiplying D27 by (1+ E65). However, the formula can not simply be copied across the remainder of the row because all of the co-ordinates have been given as RELATIVE locations. For example, if we were to copy the formula from D27 over to E27, it would appear as: (D27*(1+F65)). Obviously, this would be incorrect since the formula would no longer point to E65, the location of the growth rate data.

To overcome this, we must fix E65 as an ABSOLUTE co-ordinate, one that will not change when the formula is copied to another location. This is done by editing the formula in D27 so that it now appears as: (C27*(1+$E$65)). The dollar signs fix both parts of the co-ordinate so that they will not change. Make this change by moving over to D27 and pressing F2 so that the cell contents can be edited.

The formula can now be copied across the range E27..N27.

* Move to D27 and select "Copy" from the main menu. Press Enter to mark D27 as the block to be copied.

* Move to E27 and press the "." to mark this as the start of the block to copy to.

* Move to N27 and press Enter, marking this as the end of the block to copy to and completing the copying operation.

If you examine the contents of the cells you have just copied, you will now find that the E65 co-ordinate has remained constant. For example, the formula for June appears as (G27*(1+$E$65)) and the formula for December as (M27*(1+$E$65)).

The value of each month's sales can be calculated by multiplying the quantity sold by the current selling price. The initial selling price was set in C63, when we entered our series of initial values. Thus, the formula for the value of January's sales is: (C64*C63). Note that the figure for the number of items sold is also taken from the area containing the starting values. An alternative would be to use C27 in the formula since this is an exact copy of the value stored in C64. Enter the formula into C28, January's "Sales (£)".

Once more, the formula can not be copied across the remainder of the row since C63 is a RELATIVE co-ordinate. For example, copying the formula into D28 (February's figure) would result in: (D64*D63). In order to fix C63 as an ABSOLUTE co-ordinate, we must edit the formula in C28 so that it now appears as: (C64*$C$63). Move to C28 and press F2 so that you can do this now.

The formula can now be copied across the remainder of the row.

* Move to C28 and select "Copy" from the main menu. Press Enter to mark C28 as the block to be copied.

* Move to D28 and press the "." to mark this as the start of the block to copy to.

* Move to N28 and press Enter, marking this as the end of the block to copy to and completing the copying operation.

Thanks to the preparations made earlier, only a very simple formula is needed to calculate the income from MegaWidget's investment. You will recall that we divided the annual interest rate by 12 to obtain its monthly equivalent. We then divided the monthly equivalent by 100 to obtain a decimal fraction. The amount of the investment can now be multiplied by the decimal fraction to produce the amount of interest earned each month. If the size of the investment is stored in C70 and the decimal fraction is stored in E72, the necessary formula will be: (C70*E72).

Without the preliminary calculations made earlier, we would need to use the annual interest rate stored in C71 in this formula: (C70*((C71/12)/100)). Since the formula is intended to be copied across the rest of the row, it would be unnecessarily repetitive and complicated.

On this occasion, both co-ordinates need to be given as ABSOLUTE references. The reason for this is because the same amount of interest will be received each month. Thus, the formula must be changed so that it becomes: ($C$70*$E$72). Enter this formula into C29 and then copy it across the remainder of the row using the steps given earlier.

Having completed the "Cash Inflows" section of the cash flow forecast, we can now enter a subtotal calculation so that we can test the accuracy of the worksheet. Note that the subtotal calculation should be seen as provisional entry in the worksheet since the formula may need to be altered or removed altogether at a later date.

There is a built-in function for adding together all of the values in a given range. The syntax for this command is:

```
@SUM(Range)
```

In our case, we need to add together the values in C27, C28 and C29. Thus, the formula becomes: @SUM(C27..C29). Enter this at C31.

This time, the use of RELATIVE co-ordinates means that copying the formula to, say, D31 will result in: @SUM(D27..D29) - the correct formula for a subtotal of February's cash inflows. Copy C31 to the range D31..N31.

We can use the @SUM function as a handy cross-reference, to work out an annual total for sales in units, sales in £s and interest received on the investment. Move to P27 and enter the formula: @SUM(C27..N27). This gives us an annual total for the number of items sold. Now copy the formula to P28 and P29, giving annual totals for sales in £s and interest received. Finally, copy the formula to P31, which will give the total income for year. As you will see, the co-ordinates in each copy of the formula have changed so that each calculation is correct.

At this point, the worksheet now looks like this:

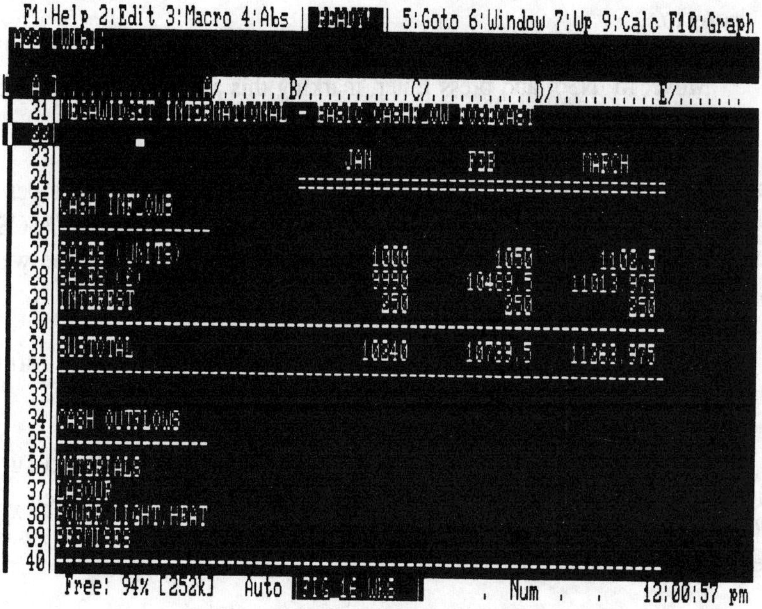

5.14 Calculating the Cash Outflows.

We can move along a little more rapidly now to complete the rest of the calculations needed for the worksheet.

Since materials are calculated on a per-unit basis, the total cost of each month's materials is obtained by multiplying the number of units sold by the unit cost. The position of the unit cost in the worksheet is fixed, meaning that co-ordinates must be specified as ABSOLUTE locations if the formula is to be copied into other locations. The materials unit cost is stored at C66 in the starting values area of the worksheet and the number of items sold in January is given in C27. Therefore, the formula that should be used is: (C27*$C$66).

Enter this formula into C36 and copy it across the range D36..N36 as follows:

- * Move to C36 and select "Copy" from the main menu. Press Enter to mark C36 as the block to be copied.

* Move to D36 and press the "." to mark this as the start of the block to copy to.

* Move to N36 and press Enter, marking this as the end of the block to copy to and completing the copying operation.

Labour costs are calculated in exactly the same way except that the cost per unit is located at C67 instead of C66. The formula now becomes: (C27*$C$67). Enter this at C37 and copy it across the range D37..N37 in the same way as shown above.

The power, heat and light unit cost is located at C68, giving the formula: (C27*$C$68). Enter this at C38 and copy it across the range D38..N38.

The final cost, rental, is a fixed monthly amount that needs no further manipulation. Copy this value directly from the starting values area (C69) into C39 with: ($C$69). Copy C39 across the range D39..N39 just as you have copied the other formulas in this section.

We can now produce a series of sub-totals to check the accuracy of the formulas in the Cash Outflows area. Once more, we will use the @SUM function to add together all of the values in a specified range. The first sub-total will produce the total annual cost of materials by adding together all of the monthly costs. These values are stored in the range C36..N36, giving a formula of: @SUM(C36..N36). Enter this formula at P36 and copy it to the range P37..P39, giving similar sub-totals for annual labour, power and rental costs.

The second set of sub-totals gives the total cash outflow for each month. This is done by adding together the values in the range C36..C39 with the formula: @SUM(C36..C39). Enter this formula at C41 and copy it across the range D41..N41.

The worksheet should now appear as:

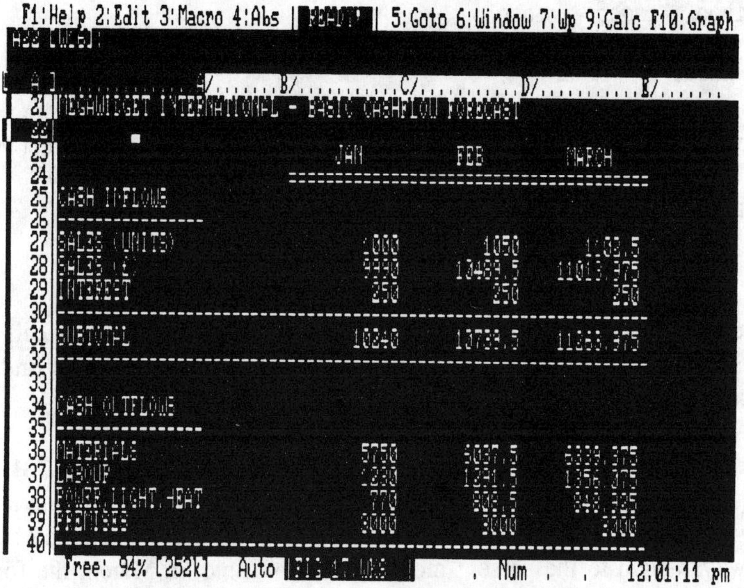

5.15 Calculating the monthly balance.

All that remains now is to produce a monthly balance based on all of the cash inflows and outflows recorded in the worksheet.

January's balance is the simplest to obtain since it involves merely subtracting the cash outflows sub-total from the cash inflows sub-total. The cash inflows sub-total is located at C31 and the cash outflows subtotal is at C41. Thus, the formula to be entered at C45 is: (C31-C41).

In February, we must take account of any surplus or deficit of cash arising from the transactions carried out in January. This can be done by adapting the formula slightly so that January's balance is added to the figure for February. This will produce the correct result regardless of whether or not January's balance is negative or positive.

Take the following example: January's balance is £1000, February's cash inflow is £3000 and February's cash outflow is £1000. This gives a calculation of:

```
January's balance + February's cash inflows - February's cash
outflows
```

£1000 + £3000 - £1000

= £2000

If January's balance is negative, this formula will still produce the correct result:

-£1000 + £3000 - £1000

= £1000

If you doubt this, try it out with a pocket calculator or use an empty cell in the worksheet itself (remembering to enclose the calculation in brackets and omit the currency symbol from each number).

In the cash flow forecast, the formula for February becomes: (C45+D31-D41). Enter this at D45 and then copy D45 across the range E45..N45. Note that the co-ordinates in the formula change eac time, so that the previous month's balance is always added to the present month's. For example, in March, the formula becomes (D45+E31-E41), and in December it is (M45+N31-N41).

5.16 Putting the final touches to the cash flow forecast.

There are several significant omissions from the worksheet that need to be rectified before it is complete.

Firstly, the values in the cash flow forecast have not been formatted as currency. Where the monthly balance is concerned, it is important that any negative figures are made very clear. Anyone glancing through the worksheet might easily miss the minus sign in front of some of the balance figures, mistaking a negative total for a positive one. This is far less likely to happen if negative figures are enclosed in brackets - as they would be if the cell was formatted to display currencies. The worksheet will also appear more attractive - and impressive - if it is presented in a professional manner.

Format all of the cells in the cash flow forecast by carrying out the following steps:

* Move to the first cell in the block you wish to format.

* From the main menu, select "Range"

* From the Range sub-menu, select "Format"

* From the Format sub-menu, select "Currency"

* Press Enter to accept 2 as the number of decimal places to use

* Since the cursor is already anchored, move to the last cell in the block and press Enter.

The abbreviated form of this set of commands would be: "/RFC".

See 4.11 for more information on formatting cells.

Although you could format each distinct block of cells individually, in this worksheet it will do no harm if you format the whole of the cash flow forecast section in one operation. To do this, use A28 as the start co-ordinate of the block and P46 as the end co-ordinate.

When formatting sections of the cash flow forecast, remember that the range C27..P27 should not be altered as these figures give units, not monetary values.

The second problem area concerns titles and notes. You may have noticed that some labels appear to be incomplete. The importance of accurate titles and labels has been stressed a number of times, particularly in section 5.8.

Two good examples of inaccurate labels are: "MegaWidget International - Basic Cash flow Forecast" (the title for the cash flow forecast which appears at A21), and "Selling Price" (a label which appears in the starting values section of the worksheet at A63).

In the first example, no indication is given of the period covered by the cash flow forecast. In the second, only we - the producers of the worksheet - know that the selling price must have been established in December 1992 for the forecast to cover the period between January 1993 and December 1993 - but will anyone else?

Go through all of the labels in the worksheet and change any that you consider to be incorrect. Pay particular attention to the points made at the beginning of section 5.8 and ensure that all labels are both concise and unambiguous.

Having made all of these changes, the worksheet should now appear similar to the illustration below.

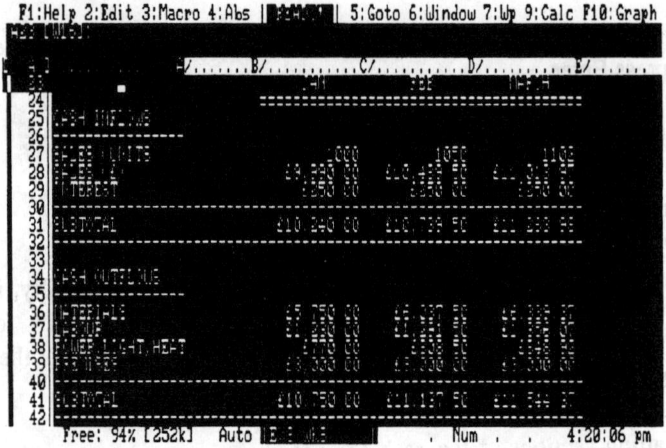

5.17 Using the spreadsheet for simple text editing

Pressing F7 from the spreadsheet program will activate a simple text editor that can be used to create text pages, including introductory screens.

Once in the text editor, there are two special keys that perform the following functions:

* F7 - This alters the JUSTIFICATION mode of the text editor, switching between RAGGED (flush left margin, uneven right margin) and JUSTIFY (both margins flush).

* F2 - This allows the RULER line to altered, so that line width and other settings can be changed.

Moving around the text editor screen is done by using the normal editing keys;

arrow keys, Backspace, Delete, Insert and so on.

When the text has been entered, pressing the Escape key returns to the main spreadsheet program. The text is automatically entered as a set of labels into the area of the screen that was displayed when the text editor was first activated. For example, if the cursor was located at A1, the page of text would be placed in the area A1..H20 (assuming that the column width had not been altered). In other words, each page of text is 20 lines deep by 80 columns wide.

5.18 Adding the introductory screen

The final amendment that must be made to the worksheet is the addition of an introductory screen for the benefit of other users. The information that should be included in an introductory screen is listed in section 5.4. A sample introductory screen is given below.

The introductory screen is clear and concise. The name and designation of the developer are given, as is the period covered by the worksheet and the title of the company. The locations of the different sections of the worksheet are present and users are informed that no macros have been created (see 6.14).

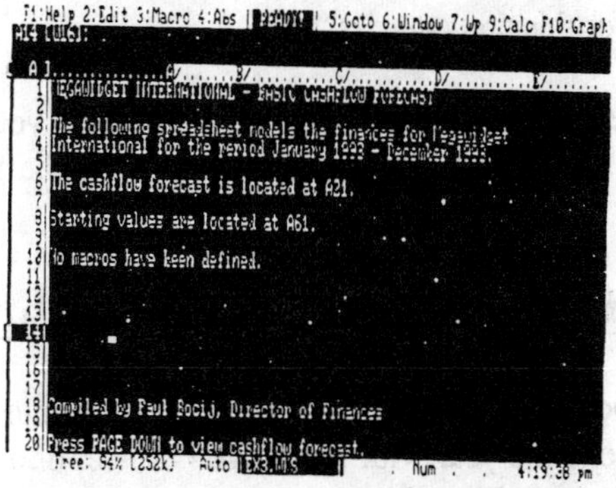

Move to A1 and press F7 to enter the program's text editing mode so that you can produce a page of text similar to the one above. Refer to the previous section for more information on how to use the text editor.

Note that in the design of the spreadsheet, it was decided that the Page Down key could be used instead of defining a series of macros (see 6.14). Thus, the introductory screen is located at the HOME position (A1). Pressing Page Down once takes the user to the cash flow forecast and pressing it again moves to the starting values section. This should serve as an excellent example of how a good preliminary design can simplify the construction of almost any worksheet.

5.19 Saving the sample worksheet

This worksheet will be used again in a later section. Save it to disk now so that you can recall it when needed. More information on file operations is contained in sections 9.8 to 9.23.

* From the main menu, select "File"

* From the File sub-menu, select "Store"

* Enter a file name of "EX2_CASH.WKS". The underscore character is obtained by holding down the Shift key and pressing "-". Notice how a meaningful file name is used; the first part refers to "Example 2" and the second part reminds you that this is a cash flow forecast.

* Press Return to save the file

The abbreviation for this procedure is "/FS".

If you have saved the file before, you may be asked if you want to REPLACE or BACKUP the file. Select "Replace", so you store the latest version of the worksheet.

5.20 Examining the company's cash flow

In the current model, the various factors we have taken into account suggest that the company will end the year with a positive balance of a little over £2,600. To demonstrate the flexibility of the design technique used here, let's simulate a radical upheaval in the state of the world widget market.

At the end of 1992, and in response to a sudden surge in demand, several major new competitors spring into the market with a range of low-cost widgets. Within months, MegaWidget finds that it is no longer a specialist supplier and is unable to lower manufacturing costs by more than a fraction. Having lost its *competitive advantage* (see 7.2), the company is now forced to concentrate on aggressive marketing in order to capture the largest possible share of the market.

The result of these changes means that the price of widgets falls from £9.99 to just £5.99. However, the company manages to negotiate a new contract with its suppliers, lowering the cost of materials to £2.75 per unit. Additionally, the new demand for widgets increases sales to 2000 units in December 1992 and the company predicts that the growth in sales will be in the region of 10% per month.

Let's see how these changes alter the company's financial position. Move to the starting values area of the worksheet and enter the following values:

```
(C63) 5.99
(C64) 2000
(C65) 10
(C66) 2.75
```

Notice how the worksheet is updated automatically with each new entry.

Now, what do these changes mean to MegaWidget's future? Far from harming the company's profits, it seems that the upheaval in the market will cause it to end the year with a positive balance of more than £20,000. Thus, MegaWidget need not take a more aggressive stance towards its competitors since it will benefit more from their presence than from their absence.

The purpose of this example is to show the built-in flexibility of worksheets designed according to the techniques described in this section. With just four minor alterations, we have been able to simulate an extreme set of circumstances and make a relatively sophisticated analysis. However, our "what if?" questioning can also be applied to more basic concerns. Try altering the starting values in the worksheet to see how you might answer some of the "what if?" questions below.

* What if we increased wages by the rate of inflation?

* What if we moved to cheaper premises?

* What if we negotiated a discount on materials or found a cheaper supplier?

* What if we increased prices?

* What if we invested some our profits elsewhere or bought more equipment?

* What if sales fell due to a recession?

Any changes you make will only be temporary since a copy of the original worksheet is stored safely on disk. If the worksheet becomes almost unrecognisable, you may want to load a fresh copy of it from disk.

* Select "File" from the main menu

* Select "Retrieve" from the File sub-menu

* Move the highlight bar to the file name "EX2_CASH.WKS"

* Press Enter to load the file

The abbreviation for this procedure is "/FR".

5.21 Creating related applications

The principles and techniques used in the creation of the cash flow forecast can be applied to a wide range of other applications without the need for any further knowledge. As an example, let's take a look at how you might create a worksheet to balance a cheque book.

The worksheet would be divided into two main sections; deposits and withdrawals. Only one starting value would be needed (an opening balance) and transactions would be added or subtracted from a running total. In its simplest form, the worksheet would contain a single area consisting of columns for transaction number, date, payee, amount and balance. All transactions would be entered into the same column; withdrawals as negative numbers and deposits as positive numbers. This way, the same basic formula could be used to calculate a new balance figure after each transaction.

A more sophisticated approach would be to create two separate storage areas within the worksheet, using one for withdrawals and the other for deposits. At the end of each month, the total deposits could be added to the opening balance and the total withdrawals could be subtracted. However, unlike the cruder method described above, this system would be unable to show individual events and might give a false view of the status of the account. For example, this method would be unable to show if the account went overdrawn in the middle of the month but ended up in credit.

The diagram below shows how the worksheet for a cheque book account might appear.

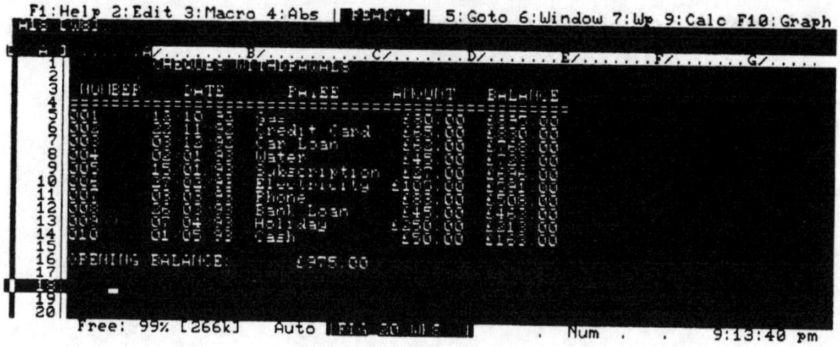

Although we have only looked at a very small set of formulas and calculations, the cheque book example should help to illustrate how these can be used to create a range of relatively sophisticated applications. Here are several more examples of worksheets that can be created using basic addition, subtraction, division and multiplication:

* Bookkeeping systems

* Personal tax calculations

* Simple statistical analysis

* Scoring systems (e.g. credit scoring)

* Simple financial analysis, such as ratio analysis

* Budgeting

5.22 Summary

In this section, you have learned how to:

* Design a worksheet
* Use titles and labels
* Use an introductory screen
* Establish a set of starting values for a worksheet
* Simplify the structure of a worksheet
* Enter calculations and formulas into a worksheet
* Fix co-ordinates as absolute locations
* Copy values into a cell
* Use the program's built-in text editor
* Perform simple "what if?" calculations

Section 6: Graphs, Reports and Macros

6.1 Objective

Part of a spreadsheet's strength lies in its ability to process data and produce meaningful information in the form of graphs or reports. The visual representation of information can make a situation easier to understand and adds impact to any kind of presentation. A printed report provides a fixed source of reference and can be used to substantiate decisions.

In a company, graphs, charts and reports help to document the decision-making process. On a smaller scale, a dazzling report might impress a small businessman's banker or clarify an uncertain area of business. In short, a graph or report shows almost any given situation from a different perspective and makes it easier to understand.

The next exercise is divided into two parts. The first part serves three purposes; to reinforce some of the skills learned earlier, to help prepare readers for the major exercise in the next section and to illustrate the use of graphs and reports. The second part serves a similar set of purposes but is geared towards a more practical application.

6.2 Generating random numbers

The built-in function "@RAND" produces a pseudo-random number, expressed to a number of decimal places (governed by the width of the current cell). For example, a typical product of the function might be: 0.110362.

To generate a random number above 1, a little multiplication must be used. For example, to generate a random number between 0 and 9, the formula "(@RAND*10)" could be used. Similarly, to generate a random number between 0 and 99, the formula "(@RAND*100) would be applied.

However, these formulas produce numbers containing several decimal places. For example, "(@RAND*100)" might return a number such as: 21.39226. An integer can be produced by applying the "@INT" function to the formula. This function strips a value of its decimal places and returns an integer. It can be applied to a random number by using a formula such as "@INT(@RAND*100)". In the previous example, the amended formula would now return a result of 23.

Occasionally, it may be necessary to avoid generating numbers that might contain zero. This can be done by adding 1 to the result of the "@RAND" section of the formula. For example, "@INT(@RAND*100)+1 would return a value between 1 and 100.

In summary:

* @RAND - returns a random number that is always less than 1

* (@RAND*XX) - returns a random number, including decimaln places, between 0 and XX-1

* @INT(RAND*XX) - returns an integer between 1 and XX

6.3 Building the sample worksheet

This worksheet relies upon the use of random numbers to generate a set of values that can be used to plot a graph with. At a later stage, we will add a relatively complex macro to the worksheet, to automate the process of viewing a range of graphs.

From this point onwards, fewer step-by-step instructions will be given. Readers should have become familiar enough with the spreadsheet program by now to be able to understand commands given as sets of keystroke sequences. However, where readers may still be a little doubtful, step-by-step instructions will continue to be given.

If the current worksheet is not empty, begin by clearing the work area as follows:

* From the main menu, select "WorkSheet"

* From the WorkSheet sub-menu, select "Erase"

* From the Erase sub-menu, select "Yes" to delete the current worksheet

Alternatively, use the command sequence "/WEY".

I. Begin the new worksheet by entering the title, "Graph and Macro Exercise", as a label at A1. Use a single quote to precede a row of equality signs in A2 and underline the title with them.

II. Fill A5 with a row of minus signs, remembering to use "\-" rather than entering the whole line manually. Copy this across the range B5..K5. Copy the same cell to the ranges A7..K7, A9..K9 and A11..K11.

III. At A4 enter "LABELS" as a normal label. At B4, enter a centred label of "One". In C4, enter "Two" and continue across the row until you reach "Ten" at K4. Remember that a label can be centred by preceding it with a "^" character.

IV. Adjust the column width at A1 from the default value of 9 to 15. Use the command sequence "/WCS" to do this. Enter the labels "X Random Data" at A6, "Y Random Data" at A8 and "Y1 Random Data" at A10.

V. Enter the formula "@INT(@RAND*100)+1" at B6, to generate a random number between 1 and 100 (see 6.2). Copy this formula across the ranges C6..K6, B8..K8 and B10..K10. Having done this, press F9 (Recalc - recalculate the worksheet) a few times to see how all of these values change each time the program updates the worksheet.

Here's how the worksheet should now look:

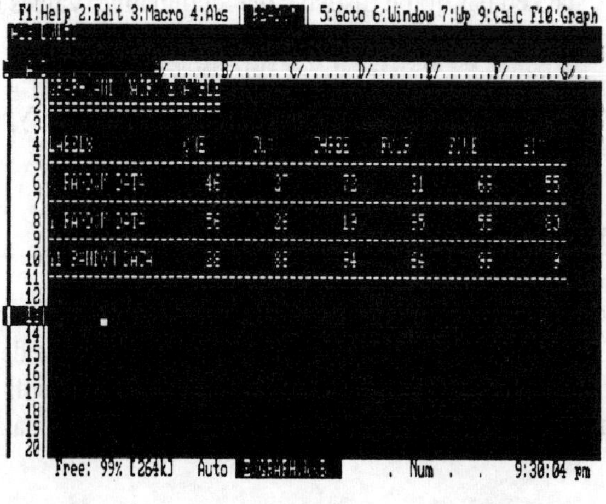

6.4 Types of graph

There are nine types of graph available in AsEasyAs. Other programs will contain most, if not all, of the graph types described here. Since several of the graph types available are intended for specialised use, only the most common are described:

* Line. All X values are treated as labels for the X axis. The scale for the Y axis is calculated automatically, according to the largest value in the data range.

* Y values are presented as a function of X, that is, Y=f(X). If the X data range contains labels, the X co-ordinate will be treated as if it were zero. The program automatically calculates a scale for the Y axis, based on the maximum value in the data range. The X axis will be equally spaced.

* Bar. All X values are treated as labels for the X axis. The width of the bars shown on the screen is determined by the number of Y values to be plotted; the fewer the values, the wider each bar.

* Pie. All X values are treated as labels. The values in the "A" data range are shown as portions of the "pie". The program is able to display sections of the pie as percentage values and can also produce exploding pie graphs.

* Stack. A stacked bar graph displays the cumulative values of a set of Y data ranges.

The type of graph to be displayed is chosen by selecting "Type" from the "Graphics" sub-menu. The keystroke sequence for this is: "/GT".

6.5 Displaying a graph

The procedure for displaying a simple graph is very straightforward. However, it is important to remember that most graphs use the data range defined for the X axis as labels. The program's automatic scaling function will be adequate in most cases since this is based on the largest value in the Y axis data range.

* Select “Graphics” from the main menu

* Select “Type” from the Graphics sub-menu. Choose which type of graph you wish to use.

* Select “X” from the Graphics sub-menu and mark the range of values to be used for the X axis.

* Select “A” from the Graphics sub-menu and mark the range of values to be used for the Y axis.

* Mark any further sets of values to be plotted on the Y axis by using the Graphics sub-menu options labelled “B” to “F”.

* Select “View” to display the graph

* After viewing the graph, press any key to return to the Graphics sub-menu

Once a graph has been defined, the F10 key will allow the graph to be viewed at any time. This is the equivalent of selecting “View” from the Graphics sub-menu.

6.6 Adding titles to a graph

As well as being able to give graphs a main title, it is also possible to label curves, the X axis, the Y axis and data ranges. To create a main title:

* Select “Graphics” from the main menu

* Select “Options” from the Graphics sub-menu

* Select “Titles” from the Options sub-menu

* Select “First” from the Titles sub-menu

* Type the main title for the graph and press Enter

The abbreviation for this sequence of commands is: “/GOTF”. A secondary title and labels for the X and Y axis can also be entered from the Titles sub-menu. Ranges can be labelled by selecting "Labels" from the Graphics sub-menu ("/GL"). Curve legends can be entered by selecting "Options" from the Titles sub- menu ("/GOL").

If a "Reset" option is available in a particular sub-menu, this can be used to delete a label or title automatically. Alternatively, the label can be erased manually by entering a blank (empty) label.

6.7 Displaying a sample graph

As you should already know, most of the graphs in AsEasyAs and other packages use the data defined for the X range as a set of labels for the X axis. In our sample data, we have already created a set of labels that can be used for our graph.

* Move to B4 and select "Graphics" from the main menu

* Select "X" from the Graphics sub-menu

* Highlight the range B4..K4 and press Enter

* Press Escape several times to return to the worksheet

Having selected a set of labels for the X axis, now define two sets of random data for plotting against the Y axis.

* Move to B6 and select "Graphics" from the main menu

* Select "A" from the Graphics sub-menu

* Highlight the range B6..K6 and press Enter

* Press Escape several times to return to the worksheet

Repeat this process using "B" to indicate the second set of Y values and highlighting B8..K8 as the data range to use. You should notice that there is no need to return to the worksheet each time you highlight a range, since each operation returns you to the Graphics sub-menu.

The program has now been given sufficient information for it to be able to generate a graph.

* Select "Graphics" from the main menu

* Select "Type" from the Graphics sub-menu

* Select "Bar" as the type of graph for the program to display

* Select "View" to see the graph on the screen

* When you have finished looking at the graph, press any key to return to the Graphics sub-menu

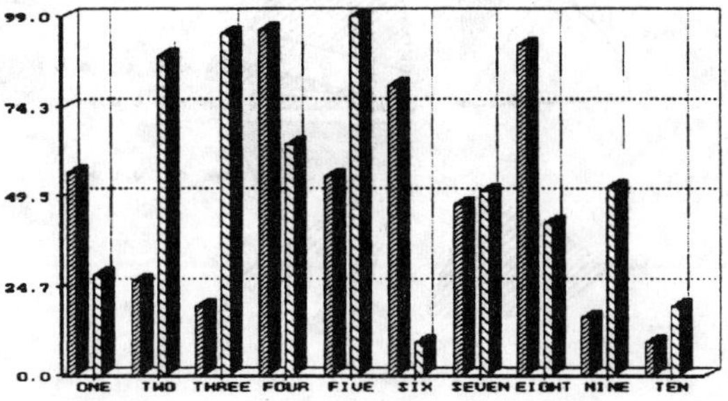

Using the command sequence "/GT", select graph types of Stacked, Area and Pie. View these by pressing "V" from the Graphics sub-menu. Although the data used for each graph will vary (since a new set of random numbers is generated each time), the graphs should appear roughly as shown by the following diagrams.

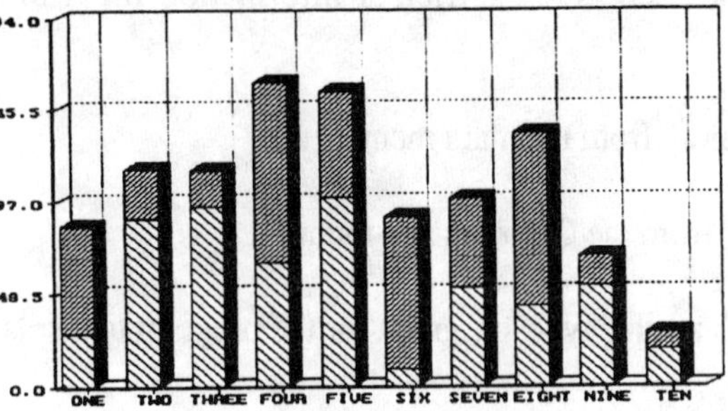
194.0
145.5
97.0
48.5
0.0
ONE
TWO
THREE
FOUR
FIVE
SIX
SEVEN
EIGHT
NINE
TEN

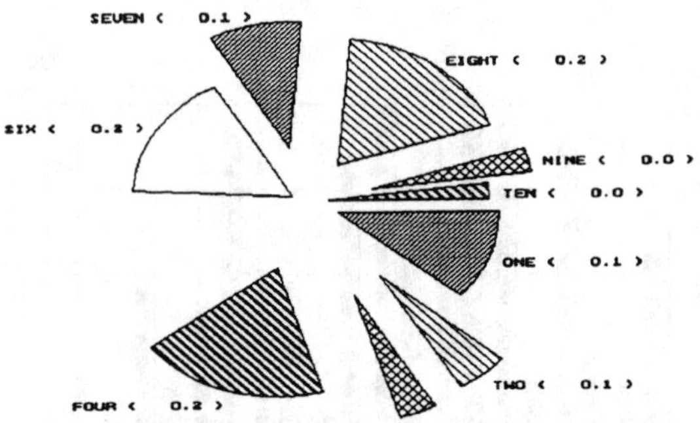
SEVEN (0.1)
EIGHT (0.2)
SIX (0.2)
NINE (0.0)
TEN (0.0)
ONE (0.1)
TWO (0.1)
FOUR (0.2)

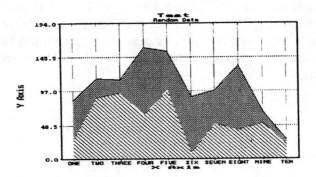

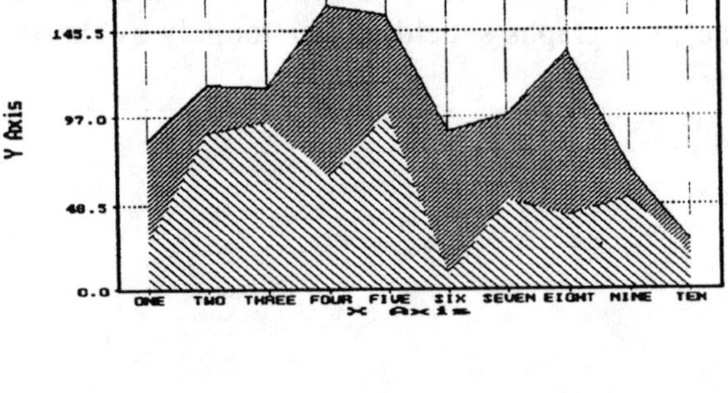
Test
Random Data
194.0
145.5
97.0
48.5
0.0
Y Axis
ONE
TWO
THREE
FOUR
FIVE
SIX
SEVEN
EIGHT
NINE
TEN
X Axis

Although all of these graphs are quite attractive, it would be more impressive if we could add a set of titles to them.

* Select "Graphics" from the main menu

* Select "Options" from the Graphics sub-menu

* Select "Titles" from the Options sub-menu

* Select "First" from the Titles sub-menu and enter "Test" as a main title

* Select "Second" from the Titles sub-menu and enter "Random Data" as a subtitle

* Select "X" from the Titles sub-menu and enter "X Axis" as a title for the X axis

* Select "Y" from the Titles sub-menu and enter "Y Axis" as a title for the Y axis

Now, press Escape twice, so that you return to the Graphics sub-menu and once again select "View" to see each type of graph. Remember to use "Type" so that you can swap between Pie, Bar, Area and Stacked.

If you experiment with other types of graph, you will notice that some are not displayed properly. This is because they require a set of values to be specified for the X axis (as opposed to a set of labels). From the Graphics sub-menu, select "X" and press Escape until the pre-selected range of cells is cleared. Move to B6 and mark the range B6..K6; the "X Random Data" range. Now try viewing some or all of the graphs again. If you want to view some of the earlier graphs, simply replace the X data range with B4..K4 again.

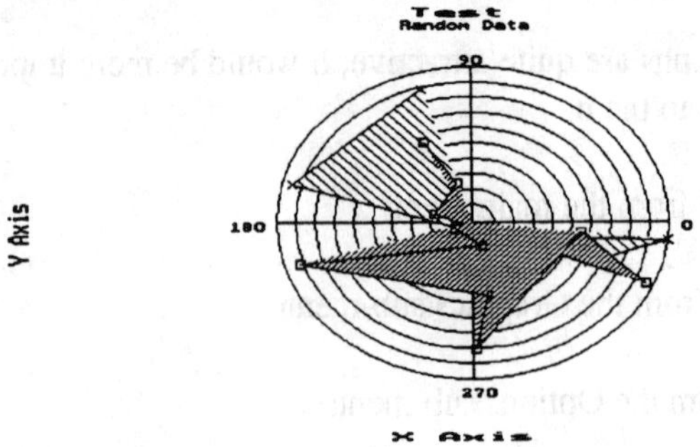

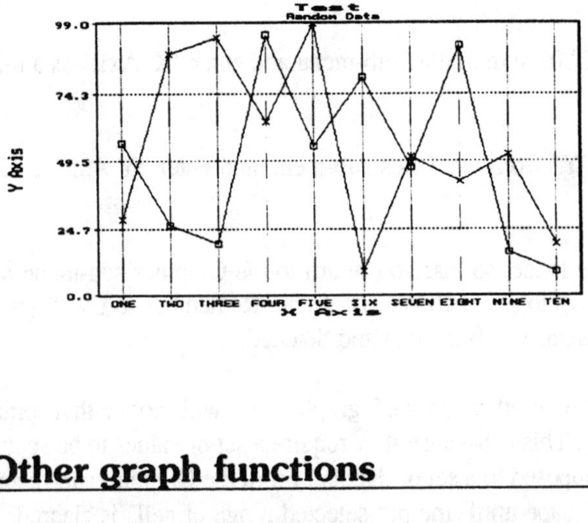

6.8 Other graph functions

There are several ways in which graphs can be enhanced. The functions described below are available from the Graphics sub-menu. This is accessed by pressing "/" to summon the main menu and then selecting the option labelled "Graphics".

* It is possible to overlay a grid on any graph by using the command sequence "/GOG". The Grid sub-menu allows you to specify various settings for the grid, such as solid or dotted lines.

* The program's automatic scaling feature can be disabled by using the command sequence "/GOS" to reach the Scale sub-menu. You can set

both the X axis and Y axis scales manually, selecting upper and lower limits, the number of steps along the axis and several other options.

* The Formats sub-menu can be used to alter the way each curve is shown on the graph. You can choose to show lines, symbols or both and whether or not "depth" should be used when displaying bars. This menu is accessed with the sequence "/GOF".

* The Colour sub-menu can be used to toggle between a colour and monochrome display; ideal for machines with LCD screens or monochrome monitors (for example, systems with Hercules display cards). This menu is accessed with "/GOC". On colour systems, users are given the choice of using solid fills or patterns. To make this a little clearer, the illustrations in this book use pattern fills.

6.9 Using named views

The Name sub-menu gives access to a number of extremely powerful features. Once a graph has been created, it can be given a name and saved to disk. At any time, this data can be loaded back into the program and the graph can be displayed immediately. If several graphs have been defined for the same worksheet, two named views can be displayed simultaneously, one overlaid upon the other. It is also possible to display two graphs separately, using the "Split" command.

To name the current graph or view a named graph:

* Select "Graphics" from the main menu

* Select "Name" from the Graphics sub-menu

* Select "Use" from the Name sub-menu. If any named graphs already exist, a selector box will appear. You can choose the graph you wish to use by highlighting its name with the cursor keys and pressing Enter.

* If you wish to name a new graph, ignore the selector box (if it appears) and simply type the name for the new graph. Press Enter when you have finished to accept the new name.

* Once you have chosen a named graph to view, select "View" from the Graphics sub-menu or press F10 from the main screen to display the graphic.

The data concerning a named graph is stored when it is named. This removes the need to set scales, titles and other information whenever you want to display a different kind of graph.

To save a named view to disk:

Follow the instructions given above, selecting "Create" instead of "Use" in the third step. The view will be named and the graph information will be stored to disk permanently.

To delete a named view:

* Select "Graphics" from the main menu

* Select "Name" from the Graphics sub-menu

* Select "Delete" from the Name sub-menu

* Select the name of the view you want to erase and then press Enter

To overlay one graph over another:

* Select "Graphics" from the main menu

* Select "Name" from the Graphics sub-menu

* Select "Merge" from the Name sub-menu

* Select the name of the graph to be superimposed over the current graph

View the graphs in the normal way.

To display two graphs simultaneously:

* Select "Graphics" from the main menu

* Select "Name" from the Graphics sub-menu

* Select "Split" from the Name sub-menu

* Select the name of the second graph to be displayed

View the graphs in the normal way.

To reset the Merge and Split functions:

* Select "Graphics" from the main menu

* Select "Name" from the Graphics sub-menu

* Select "Reset" from the Name sub-menu

6.10 More sample graphs

Before moving on to reports and macros, we will use the sample worksheet to display merged and split graphs.

* Using the sample worksheet, set up a stacked bar graph and display it. Use the "Colour" sub-menu to display solid fill patterns (See 6.8 or use the sequence "/GOCY").

* Move to the Graphics menu and select "Name"

* Select "Create" and enter "Stack" as the name of the graph

* Set up bar and area graphs in the same way and name these "Bar" and "Area" respectively. Use the "Colour" sub-menu to ensure that these graphs are displayed using pattern fills ("/GOCN").

Since the area graph was displayed last, it is now the current graph. Test this by viewing it from the main work screen by pressing F10. If, for any reason, the area graph is not displayed, return to the Name sub- menu and choose "Use" to specify that the area graph should be used as the current view.

* Return to the Name sub-menu again and select "Merge". Use the arrow

keys to highlight "Stack" (the name of the stacked bar graph) and press Enter.

* Press Escape several times until you are returned to the main screen. Now press F10 to view the merged graphs. The display should appear similar to the picture below.

Notice that although the scales used appear to be correct, the labels along the X axis and the grid are blurred somewhat. This can be rectified by removing the grid or label data from one or both of the views. The solid and pattern fills used make each part of the graph clearly distinguishable.

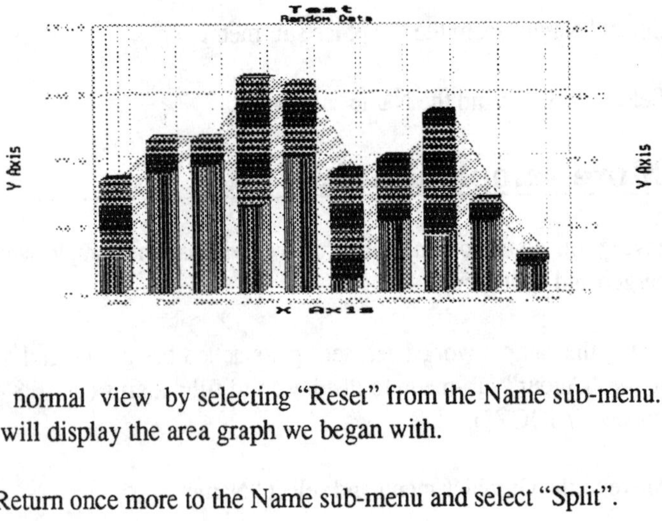

Restore a normal view by selecting "Reset" from the Name sub-menu. Pressing F10 now will display the area graph we began with.

* Return once more to the Name sub-menu and select "Split".

* Use the cursor keys to highlight "Bar" (the name of the bar graph) and press Enter

* Press Escape several times to return to the main screen and then press F10 to view the split graphs.

The display should appear similar to the picture below.

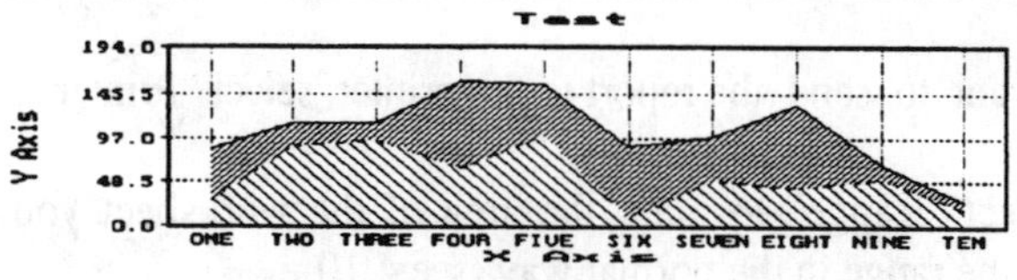

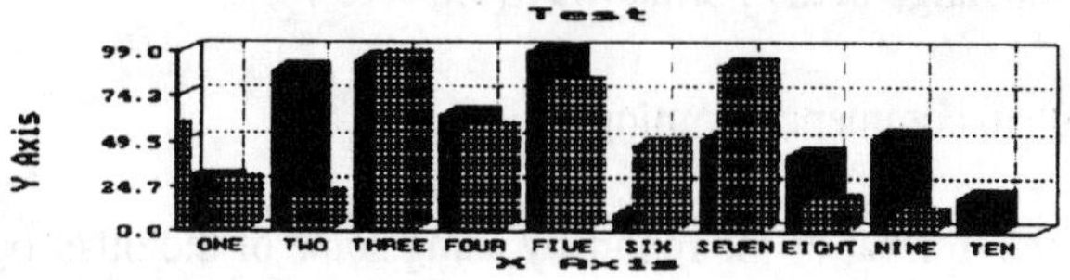

6.11 Printing reports

There are two basic types of reports available from within the program.

* As-Seen. The worksheet is printed exactly as it appears on the screen. For example, only the results of formulas are shown, not the formulas themselves.

* Contents. The contents of each cell, including format information, is printed in list format.

Obviously, the majority of as-seen worksheets will be far wider than the screen. The program overcomes this by printing the worksheet in sections, intelligently fitting as much information as possible onto each page. Additionally, users can specify a range of cells to be printed and can suppress the printing of any blank areas in the worksheet.

It is also possible to print a report to disk, as a standard ASCII text file. The file can be loaded into a word processor or other program, edited and then printed.

To print a report:

* Select "PrintTo" from the main menu

* If you want to print the report to disk, select "File" as the destination. Enter a file name for the report. Under normal circumstances, the file name extension used should be ".ASC" or ".TXT". For example, "CASHFLOW.ASC" or "CASHFLOW.TXT".

* If you want to send the report to the printer, select "Printer"

* Next, select "Range" to mark the area of the worksheet you want to print. Mark the range in the normal way (see 4.10).

* Select "Go" to commence printing

You can modify the format of the report by using some of the other options in the Print menu.

* Border allows you to fix a range of cells as a main title or set a column as the left margin for the report

* Linefeed, Adjust and Page Advance can be used to move the paper in the printer so that the top of the page can be aligned properly

* The Options sub-menu sets various options such as headers, footers, page length, margins and type of report (as-seen or contents). This menu can also be used to enter printer control codes, so that text effects can be produced on the target printer

Installing a printer for use with the program is done by entering a set of control codes. The control codes will be found in the reference section of your printer manual. All of the codes must be entered as decimal values. For example, on an Epson-compatible printer, the sequence "ESC E" switches on emphasised print and "ESC F" switches it off. The "ESC" command instructs the printer to accept the command that follows. Converting these commands to decimal values, we obtain "\027\070". If you examine your printer manual, you will find that the ASCII values of ESC and E are 27 and 70 respectively. Thus, we enter "/027/070" into the program when asked for the sequence to turn emphasised print on.

If working within a GEM, Windows or similar environment, manual printer installation should be unnecessary. For example, all Windows applications will have access to the standard printer control file installed as part of the Windows environment.

Refer to the manuals for your printer and the program for more information on how to configure the software for use with your printer.

6.12 Printing graphs

To print the current graph:

* Select "Graphics" from the main menu

* Select "Plot" from the Graphics sub-menu

* The "Image" sub-menu allows you to select the vertical and horizontal size of the graph to be printed. The default settings are all at 100% and need not be changed

* The "Density" sub-menu selects high or low density printing. High density printing appears darker and produces a better quality output.

* "Hardware" allows you to choose the destination for the graph. This can be a disk file (a .PIC graphics file), a HP Laserjet-compatible printer, a 9-pin Epson-compatible printer or a 24-pin Epson- compatible printer.

* The "Paper" sub-menu is used to specify the size of the paper in the printer.

* "Orient" specifies the orientation of the print out; portrait ("tall") or landscape ("wide").

* "Eject" advances the paper in the printer to the top of the form

* "Go" sends the graph to the destination device, whether a disk file or a printer.

There are likely to be significant differences between programs, especially Windows' applications. Refer to the manuals for your printer and the program for more information on how to configure the software for use with your printer.

6.13 Some sample reports

We will now use the sample worksheet to produce two different kinds of reports. Please note that this section assumes that your printer has been installed correctly for use with the program.

* From the main menu, select "PrintTo"

* Select "Printer" from the PrintTo sub-menu

* A new sub-menu will appear and "Range" will be already highlighted. Press Enter to select this option and mark the range A1..K11

* Ensure that the printer is ready and then select "Go" to print the report

The report should appear in the format shown below:

GRAPH AND MACRO EXAMPLE

====================

LABELS	ONE	TWO	THREE	FOUR	FIVE	SIX	SEVEN
X RANDOM DATA	46	27	72	31	69	55	30
Y RANDOM DATA	56	26	19	95	55	80	47
Y1 RANDOM DATA	28	88	94	64	9	99	z51

EIGHT	NINE	TEN
16	49	35
91	16	9
42	52	19

* Feed a fresh sheet of paper into the printer and set it on-line

* Return to the "PrintTo" sub-menu and select "Options"

* Select "Type" from the Options sub-menu

* Select "Contents" from the Type sub-menu

* Select "Go" to print the report

The command sequences for these procedures are: "/PPRG" and "/PPROTCG".

The report should appear in the format shown below:

```
A1 [W15]: 'GRAPH AND MACRO EXAMPLE
D1: '
A2 [W15]: '=======================
A4 [W15]: 'LABELS
B4: ^ONE
C4: ^TWO
D4: ^THREE
E4: ^FOUR
F4: ^FIVE
G4: ^SIX
H4: ^SEVEN
I4: ^EIGHT
J4: ^NINE
K4: ^TEN
A5 [W15]: \-
B5: \-
C5: \-
D5: \-
E5: \-
F5: \-
G5: \-
H5: \-
I5: \-
J5: \-
K5: \-
A6 [W15]: 'X RANDOM DATA
B6: @INT(@RAND*100)+1
C6: @INT(@RAND*100)+1
D6: @INT(@RAND*100)+1
E6: @INT(@RAND*100)+1
F6: @INT(@RAND*100)+1
G6: @INT(@RAND*100)+1
H6: @INT(@RAND*100)+1
I6: @INT(@RAND*100)+1
J6: @INT(@RAND*100)+1
K6: @INT(@RAND*100)+1
A7 [W15]: \-
B7: \-
C7: \-
```

```
D7: \-
E7: \-
F7: \-
G7: \-
H7: \-
I7: \-
J7: \-
K7: \-
A8 [W15]: 'Y RANDOM DATA
B8: @INT(@RAND*100)+1
C8: @INT(@RAND*100)+1
D8: @INT(@RAND*100)+1
E8: @INT(@RAND*100)+1
F8: @INT(@RAND*100)+1
G8: @INT(@RAND*100)+1
H8: @INT(@RAND*100)+1
I8: @INT(@RAND*100)+1
J8: @INT(@RAND*100)+1
K8: @INT(@RAND*100)+1
A9 [W15]: \-
B9: \-
C9: \-
D9: \-
E9: \-
F9: \-
G9: \-
H9: \-
I9: \-
J9: \-
K9: \-
A10 [W15]: 'Y1 RANDOM DATA
B10: @INT(@RAND*100)+1
C10: @INT(@RAND*100)+1
D10: @INT(@RAND*100)+1
E10: @INT(@RAND*100)+1
F10: @INT(@RAND*100)+1
G10: @INT(@RAND*100)+1
H10: @INT(@RAND*100)+1
I10: @INT(@RAND*100)+1
J10: @INT(@RAND*100)+1
K10: @INT(@RAND*100)+1
A11 [W15]: \-
B11: \-
C11: \-
D11: \-
E11: \-
F11: \-
```

```
G11: \-
H11: \-
I11: \-
J11: \-
K11: \-
```

6.14 What is a macro?

A keyboard macro records a sequence of events, stores them under a given name and then replays them whenever the macro is activated. For example, typing the phrase "I look forward to hearing from you" requires more than 30 separate keystrokes. If this phrase was used often, it would probably be better to store all of these keystrokes in a macro. If this was done, pressing a key combination, such as ALT and Z, would cause the program to react in exactly the same way as if the entire phrase had been typed in manually. Thus, almost any set of repetitive keystrokes can be reduced to a single key combination by defining the entire sequence as a macro.

Depending on the capabilities of the software being used, macros can be used for far more than just abbreviating words or phrases. They can be used to access menus, copy disk files, run external programs and much more.

In a spreadsheet, sequences of macro instructions are stored in a range of cells. The range is then given a name that corresponds to the key combination required to activate the macro and the process is complete.

6.15 Defining macros

The macro key words used by any particular program will be listed in the user manual or in the program's on-line help. However, most programs support a number of common macro "words". A list of common macro key words is given in Appendix 2.

* Move to a suitable position in the worksheet and enter the macro commands you require, working downwards in the column.

* When the sequence is complete, enter the Range sub-men and "Create" a name for the range of cells containing the macro commands ("/RNC").

The name describes the key combination required to activate the macro. For example, a name of "\A" would mean that holding down the ALT key and then pressing "A" will activate the macro.

Here is an example of a macro:

* Move to A60 and enter "{GOTO}A100~" as a label

* From the main menu, select "Range", followed by "Name" and "Create"

* Enter "\A" as the name for the range

* Highlight A100 as the range to be named and press Enter

Press Home to move to A1 in the worksheet. Now press ALT and A to activate the macro (which will take you to A100 again).

6.16 A sample macro

Try the example given in the previous section before going any further. Try changing the co-ordinate (A100) to see how this affects the macro.

The sample macro that will be constructed here is designed to display three different graphs automatically. Although the instructions that follow might appear to be complex, they are really quite simple.

* Move to A14 and enter a label of "View Graphics Macro (Alt-G)"

* Underline the title in A14 by entering a line of equality signs in A15. Remember to mark this entry as a label by preceding the equality signs with a single quote.

* Enter the following data (the cell co-ordinates are given at the beginning of each line):

```
(A17) /GXB4..K4~
(A18) AB8..K8~
(A19) BB10..K10~
(A20) OTF{DEL 20}TEST~{ESC 5}
```

```
(A21) /GOTS{DEL 20}RANDOM DATA~{ESC 5}
(A22) /GOTX{DEL 20}X AXIS~{ESC 5}
(A23) /GOTY{DEL 20}Y AXIS~{ESC 5}
(A24) /GOSYS4~QQQ
(A25) OGBQ
(A26) TBV
(A27) TPV
(A28) TAV{ESC}
```

* Now enter a set of labels to describe each line of the macro:

```
(D17) SET X RANGE
(D18) SET Y RANGE
(D19) SET Y1 RANGE
(D20) SET MAIN TITLE
(D21) SET 2ND TITLE
(D22) SET X AXIS TITLE
(D23) SET Y AXIS TITLE
(D24) SET VERTICAL SCALE
(D25) SET GRID ON
(D26) VIEW BAR GRAPH
(D27) VIEW PIE CHART
(D28) VIEW AREA GRAPH
```

This section of the worksheet should now appear as:

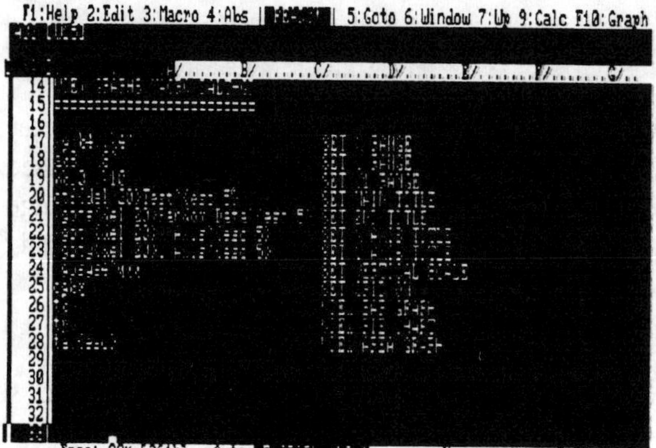

* Move to A17 and then select "Range" from the main menu

* Select "Name" from the Range sub-menu

* Select "Create" from the Name sub-menu and enter a name of "\G"

* Mark the range A17..A28 and press Enter

The abbreviation for this procedure is "/RNC".

Before activating the macro, access the Graphics sub-menu from the main menu and choose "Name". Use "Reset" in the Name sub-menu so that any split or merged graph displays are deactivated. This can be abbreviated to: "/GNR".

Activate the macro by holding down the ALT key and then pressing "G". You will see a set of menus flash up briefly and then the first graph will be displayed. Press a key and the menus will appear again for a split second before the second graph is displayed. Press a key again and the third graph will be displayed. A final key press will return you to the main screen.

We will now work through the macro commands individually, to explain in more depth how it all works. It is important to remember at all times that the sequences in the macro correspond exactly to the key presses you would make if you were carrying out these operations manually. Thus, "/GOT" is the same as pressing "/" to access the main menu, "G" to enter the Graphics sub-menu, "O" to enter the "Options" sub- menu and "T" to enter the Titles sub-menu.

```
(A17) /GXB4..K4~
```

The first line is the equivalent of pressing the keys required to enter the Graphics sub-menu and selecting "X" to define a range of cells to be used as labels for the X axis ("/GX"). The last section of the line contains the range B4..K4. The tilde (~) at the end of the line simulates the Enter key being pressed.

```
(A18) AB8..K8~
```

At this point, we would normally be returned to the Graphics sub-menu. To define a set of values to be used for the Y axis, we would press "A" and then mark a range of cells. The second line of the macro simulates this, automatically entering the range B8..K8 and terminating the line with a tilde (for "Enter").

```
(A19) BB10..K10~
```

As you might expect, the third line of the macro defines the co-ordinates for the

"B" data range (giving a second set of values for the Y axis). Again, this is the equivalent of pressing "B" in the Graphics sub-menu, defining the range B10..K10 and then pressing Enter.

```
(A20) OTF{DEL 20}TEST~{ESC 5}
```

This line is the equivalent of entering the Titles sub-menu, deleting any data already present for the first (main) title and then entering a new title of "Test".

There are three points to note here. Firstly, the section "{del 20}" uses a key word; a command that simulates a spreadsheet command. Key words are always enclosed in brackets. In this case, the key word "del" simulates the Delete key. The value of 20 entered after the key word instructs the program to react as if the Delete key was pressed 20 times.

The second point concerns the way in which the new title is entered. Notice that there is no need to surround the text with quotation marks - just as when a title is entered manually.

Finally, the "{ESC 5}" key word simulates the Escape key being pressed 5 times, returning to the main screen. This is an unnecessary action but is included to illustrate the overall sequence of events.

```
(A21) /GOTS{DEL 20}RANDOM DATA~{ESC 5}
```

This line activates the Graphics menu again, moves into the Titles sub-menu, deletes any data already present and then enters a second title of "Random Data" ("/GOTS"). Again, the title is not enclosed within quotation marks and the {ESC} key word is used to return to the main menu.

```
(A22) /GOTX{DEL 20}X AXIS~{ESC 5}
```

This line returns to the Titles sub-menu, deletes any existing title and then enters a new title of "X Axis" for the X axis.

```
(A23) /GOTY{DEL 20}Y AXIS~{ESC 5}
```

Again, we return to the Titles sub-menu, delete any existing data and enter a title of "Y Axis" for the Y axis.

```
(A24) /GOSYS4~QQQ
```

This line moves into the Options sub-menu and sets the scaling for the Y axis to 4 steps. The last part of the line, "QQQ", simulates selecting "Quit" three times, returning to the Graphics sub- menu.

```
(A25) OGBQ
```

Here, we enter the Options sub-menu once more and set the program to superimpose a horizontal and vertical grid over the graph. The final "Q" moves back up one level in the menu structure to return to the Graphics sub-menu.

```
(A26) TBV
```

This line selects "Bar" from the Type sub-menu and displays the graph.

```
(A27) TPV
```

This line selects "Pie" from the Type sub-menu and displays the graph.

```
(A28) TAV{ESC}
```

This line selects "Area" from the Type sub-menu, displays the graph and finally returns to the main screen.

If you were to go through the steps involved in displaying the three graphs manually, you would find that this macro copies all of the keys you would press exactly. There is some deliberate redundancy, such as returning to the main screen unnecessarily, and it may be worth your while seeing how you might streamline the entire operation.

6.17 Generating and analysing graphs for the sample cash flow

The random number worksheet will not be used again but you may wish to save it to disk for future reference. See 4.13 for instructions on saving and loading worksheets.

Load the sample cash flow forecast created in the last section:

* From the main menu, select "File"

* Select "Retrieve" from the File menu.

* Highlight the name "EX2_CASH.WKS" and press Enter

We will now generate some graphs that will give an at-a-glance view of the company's status throughout the year. The first graph plots MegaWidget's monthly balance over the period of the cash flow forecast.

* Select "Graphics" from the main menu

* Select "X" to enter a range of values for the X axis. Highlight the range C23..N23 (the names of the months from January - December) and press Enter.

* Select "A" to enter a range of values for the Y axis. Highlight the range C45..N45 (the balance for each month) and press Enter

* Select "Options" followed by "Titles". Enter a first title of "MegaWidget International", a second title of "Cash flow Forecast", an X axis title of "Jan - Dec 1993" and a Y axis title of "Monthly Balance"

* Press Escape once, to return to the "Graphics Options" sub-menu and select "Grid". In the Grid sub-menu, select "Both" so that a horizontal and vertical grid will be superimposed onto the graph.

* Press Escape once to return to the Graphics sub-menu and select "Type". Choose "Bar" as the type of graph to be displayed.

* Still in the Graphics sub-menu, select "Name" followed by "Create" and type the name "Balance".

* Press Escape several times, until you are returned to the main screen and then press F10 to view the graph. The graph should appear as shown below:

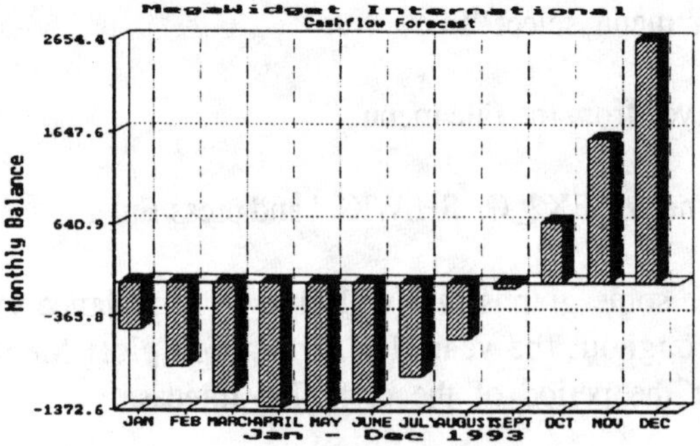

Let us make a simple analysis of the company's financial position based on the trends shown in the graph. Remember that spreadsheet models are never totally accurate; we can only ever make general predictions.

Two points become immediately apparent when the graph is examined closely. Firstly, we can predict that the company will be most vulnerable to cash flow problems throughout the period April - June 1993. Secondly, the company will only begin to operate in profit in early October.

The use of such information would allow MegaWidget's management to make important decisions regarding borrowing and investment. For example, a further modelling exercise might show that the company would be wise to consider withdrawing part of its £25000 investment so that overdraft charges could be avoided. Management staff would also be aware that the company would not be in a strong enough position to invest in more equipment until the final quarter of the year. Of course, this evidence could also be used to support applications for loans and overdrafts since the graph makes it very clear that the company will only experience short-term financial difficulties.

The next graph plots total monthly income against total monthly expenses.

* Select "Graphics" from the main menu

* Select "A" to enter a new range of values for the Y axis. Highlight the range C31..N31 (total monthly income figures for January - December) and press Enter.

* Select "B" to enter a second range of values for the Y axis. Highlight

the range C41..N41 (total monthly expenses for January - December 1993) and press Enter

* Select "Options" followed by "Titles". Change the title for the Y axis to "Income Vs Expenses"

* Press Escape once, to return to the "Graphics Options" sub-menu and select "Legend". Select "A" and enter a curve legend of "Income". Select "B" and enter a curve legend of "Expenses". This will allow the graph to display a key identifying each curve.

* Press Escape once to return to the Graphics sub-menu and select "Type". Choose "Line" as the type of graph to be displayed.

* Still in the Graphics sub-menu, select "Name" followed by "Create" and type the name "Expenses".

* Press Escape several times, until you are returned to the main screen and then press F10 to view the graph. The graph should appear as shown below:

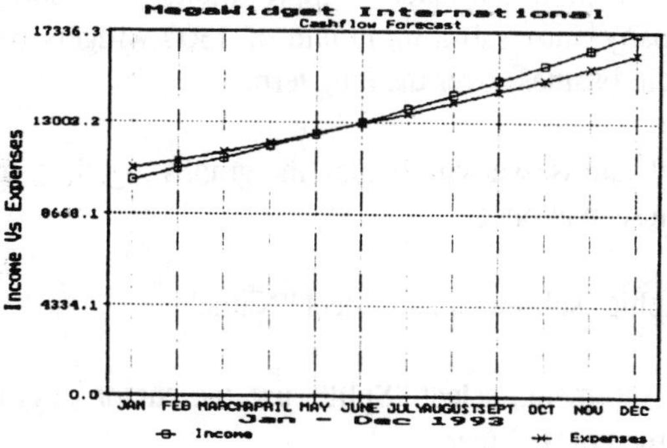

Once again, there is an important lesson to be learned from the graph. Very simply, the point at which the curves cross each other tells the company the level of sales required in order for the company to "break even". In this case, the break-even point is reached between June and July of 1993, when the value of sales first exceeds the value of expenses. Thus, the graph tells the company the minimum number of sales required each month for the company to remain in operation.

If the company were to manipulate any factors under their control (for example, selling price), it might alter the position of the break-even point to its advantage. Similarly, the graph can also be used to measure the effects of, say, a sudden rise in the cost of materials.

Here is a summary of the information that can be gleaned from these two simple graphs:

* The company will have the highest level of debt during the period April - June. With this in mind, the company should make borrowing arrangements with its bank so that it can lend approximately £1500 for a period of roughly six months. Alternatively, the company should investigate the possibility of using some of its invested capital to cope with this problem.

* The company will begin to operate in profit in the final quarter of the year, beginning in October. Only after this time should the company consider making any equipment purchases or other long- term financial commitments.

* The break-even point for sales is approximately £13000 per month. Thus, the company must sell a minimum of 1300 widgets per month in order to remain in business over the long term.

For the sake of completeness, we will display the graphs together, so that all of this information can be seen at once.

* Enter the Graphics sub-menu and select "Name"

* In the Name sub-menu, select "Split", use the cursor keys to highlight "Balance" and then press Enter

Press Escape several times until you are returned to the main screen. Press F10 to view the graph. The display should appear as shown below:

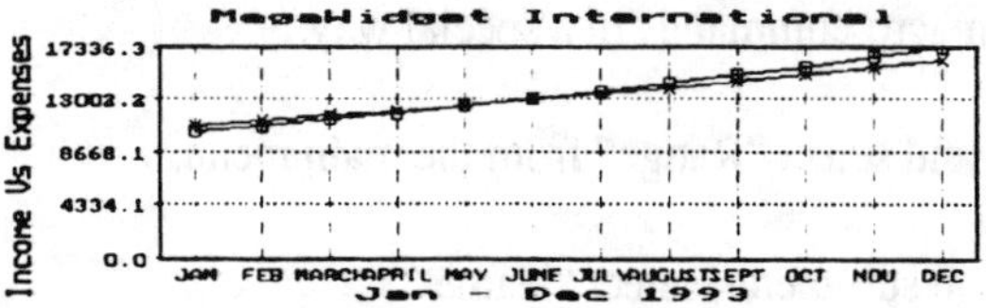

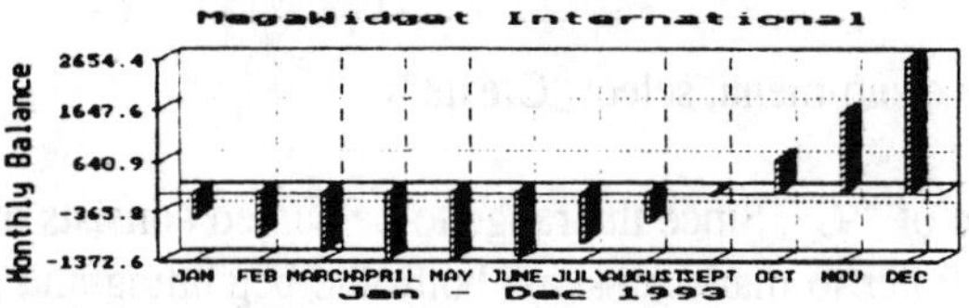

6.18 Putting finishing touches to the sample cash flow forecast

The last steps needed to complete the worksheet are a set of simple macros and a report on the contents of each cell in the worksheet. We begin by adding a few macros to make moving around the worksheet a little easier.

* Move to A81 and enter a label of "Macros". Underline this title by entering a row of equality signs in A81. Remember to precede the equality signs by a single quote (').

* Move to A84 and enter the following: {GOTO}A21~

* Move to A86 and enter: {GOTO}A61~

* Move to A88 and enter: {GOTO}A81~

* Move to B84 and enter a label along the lines of "Alt-C: Go to the cash flow forecast". Enter labels of "Alt-S: Go to the starting values area" in B61 and "Alt-M: Go to the macro area" in B81.

Notice how the labels are used to describe each function, giving both a description of the macro's purpose and its command keys. The macros themselves use the GOTO command to move to the cell co-ordinate given after the brackets. As usual, the tilde (~) represents the Enter key. At present, none of the macros are functional. This is because they have not been assigned a name for the program to recognise them by. This can be done by naming the range of cells containing the macro commands in a special way.

* Move to A84 and select "Range" from the main menu.

* From the Range sub-menu, select "Name"

* From the Name sub-menu, select "Create"

* Enter a name of "\C". Since the range to be named consists of only one cell, just press Enter to mark A84 as both the beginning and end of the range. Name A86 as "\S" and A88 as "\M" in the same way.

The abbreviated form of these commands is "/RNC".

The backwards slash (\) informs the program that the range contains a macro that is accessed by pressing ALT in combination with another key selected by the user. The three macros defined use C for "Cash flow", S for "Starting values" and M for "Macros". Test the macros to ensure that they are all working. If they do not, check that all of the commands have been entered properly or try naming them again. Remember to add details concerning the new macros to the introductory screen.

In order to make alterations to the worksheet easier to implement, it is a good idea to create a report showing the contents of every cell used.

* From the main menu, select "PrintTo"

* From the Print To sub-menu, choose "Printer" as the output device

* Select "Range" to mark the area of the worksheet for printing. In this case, the worksheet extends from A1 to P88. Mark this range.

* Select "Options" and then "Type". Choose "Contents" to print a contents report. Escape back to the Print To sub-menu by selecting "Quit" or pressing Escape.

* Make sure the printer is ready and then select "Go" to begin printing. The abbreviated form of these commands is "/PPR".

Annotate the report with your name, the file name of the worksheet ("EX2_CASH.WKS"), the title of the worksheet and the date. In future, it is a good idea to reserve some space in the worksheet so that these details can be entered as part of the model, for example as part of the introductory screen.

The cash flow worksheet will be used again in another exercise. Save the latest version of the worksheet to disk as follows:

* From the main menu, select "File"

* From the File sub-menu, select "Store"

* The name of the worksheet should appear at the top of the screen. If it is incorrect, type the name "EX2_CASH.WKS" and press Enter.

* Select "Replace" to replace the previous version of the worksheet on disk with this new one

The abbreviation for this set of commands is "/FS".

6.19 Summary

In this section, you have learned how to:

* Generate random numbers

* Plot graphs

* Define titles, labels and scales for a graph

* Define macros

* Name graphs

* View two graphs simultaneously and superimpose one graph over another

* Print graphs

* Use graphs for simple decision support

* Print reports

Section 7: Advanced Modelling

7.1 Objective

The usefulness of a spreadsheet model can be increased significantly by including the ability to interrogate the model in a variety of ways. Amongst other things, this "what if?" facility can be used to make predictions, present information to others, support management decisions, pinpoint potential problems and maximise operations.

This final exercise brings together all of the knowledge, skills and experience gained so far. The main function of the worksheet is to demonstrate how a spreadsheet can be used to model uncertainty. Additionally, a number of new skills are learned and consideration is given as to how a complex model should be presented to someone with little or no spreadsheet knowledge. For those involved in management, the exercise illustrates the use of a spreadsheet as a decision support system and its value as a tool for gaining competitive advantage.

7.2 A brief description of Competitive Advantage and Decision Support Systems

Modern businesses see accurate information as an extremely valuable resource. In the simplest of terms, information is a tool that can be used to aid competition in the marketplace, to give a company a *competitive advantage*. Although information is not necessarily obtained via Information Technology, most people associate "data" and "information" with computers.

There are various ways in which information can be used as a strategic weapon. Common methods include cutting production costs, identifying new markets, concentrating on a specialised section of the market and differentiating products from one another. Each of these tactics is successful only if timely and accurate information is available. The huge IT budgets of the most thriving companies in the world are a clear testament to the value and importance of gathering information.

It may seem obvious, but the purpose of a *decision support system* is to help management arrive at sensible decisions. A spreadsheet can be used to distill millions of pieces of data into a form that a manager can deal with quickly and efficiently. As various possibilities are considered, the spreadsheet can be used to justify some decisions whilst pointing out the flaws in others. Finally, a worksheet can be used to explain to others why a particular course of action has been chosen.

Complete descriptions of competitive advantage and decision support systems are well beyond the scope of this book. However, the importance of these areas is such that readers are referred to Appendix 5 for further reading.

7.3 Editing the cashflow worksheet

This exercise is both long and complex. In order to make the worksheet a little easier to create, you can edit the cashflow worksheet created in sections 5 and 6. If you did not save a copy of the worksheet to disk, ignore the remainder of this section and continue from 7.4.

* Load the worksheet into memory.

* Move the section containing the cashflow forecast (A21..P46) to AA1. You will need to reformat a number of columns so that they are displayed properly.

* Move the section containing the starting values (A61..F72) to A150. Copy this section to A200 so that there are now two sets of this information.

You will need to make changes to the worksheet so that it will work correctly when all of the new functions have been added. Work through the next section and make sure that your labels and formulas match those given for this exercise.

7.4 Creating the new cashflow forecast

You should already be familiar with copying, moving and formatting operations. The construction of this worksheet relies heavily on these skills. Refer to the earlier exercises for more information on these operations. As you build the worksheet, ignore any error messages that may appear in cells from time to time:

these will all be rectified when the worksheet is complete.

A complete listing of this worksheet is given in Appendix 4. Refer to this is you are unclear about the contents of any particular cell or are encountering errors.

To reduce the amount of data entry needed to create this worksheet, it has been designed so that the worksheet used in an earlier exercise can be edited and used here. However, one of the disadvantages of this is that it has been necessary to create two sets of starting values. In turn, this leads to the following problems:

* the spreadsheet will need to make a number of unnecessary calculations, reducing its peformance slightly

* more calculations and non-essential areas give a greater chance of introducing errors into the worksheet

* the overall layout of the worksheet is made more complex than it need be, leading to the possibility of confusion and maintenance problems

The normal development process of the worksheet has been bypassed so that readers can create a fully working application in the shortest possible time. The purpose of this exercise is to demonstrate the capabilities of the spreadsheet program and to illustrate several important concepts. Providing each entry is correct, when the worksheet has been completed, it will appear to work almost miraculously. In reality, this would only happen if meticulous attention had been given to planning and design before execution.

Although the worksheet represents a fully functional model, it is far from complete. A variety of simplifications have been made that would be unacceptable in the "real" world of industry. For example, you should already have noticed that the forecasts used so far assume that all monies due are received in the same month. No attempt has been made to account for credit periods, late payments and bad debts. Similarly, if the company goes overdrawn, no charges are levied by banks or other lenders. However, the design techniques shown throughout this book can be used to create worksheets flexible enough to allow these kinds of modifications to be made quickly and easily. For example, section 7.7 shows how a look up table can be used to account for random factors. With prior thought, there is no reason why a similar technique could not be applied to dealing with credit periods, discounts and bank charges.

7.5 Entering the starting values

As you should recall, one of the first sections of the worksheet should be the area containing starting values. Enter the following labels:

```
(A150) "Starting Values For MegaWidget Cashflow Forecast".
Underline this with a row of minus signs at A151.
(A152) "Selling Price"
(A153) "Starting Sales"
(A154) "Sales Growth P.M."
(A155) "Materials Cost P.U."
(A156) "Labour Cost P.U."
(A157) "Power Cost P.U."
(A158) "Monthly Rental"
(A159) "Savings Account"
(A160) "Interest Rate P.A."
(D152) "ú"
(D153) "Units"
(D154) "% Giving"
(D155) "ú"
(D156) "ú"
(D157) "ú"
(D158) "ú"
(D159) "ú"
(D160) "% - OR"
(D161) "Giving"
(F160) "% Per Month"
```

Enter the following formulas and values, ignoring any error messages that may be generated for the moment:

```
(C152) +BD3
(C153) +BD4
(C154) 5
(C155) +BD5
(C156) +BD6
(C157) +BD7
(C158) 3000
(C159) 25000
(C160) +BD9
(E154) (C154/100)
(E160) (C160/12)
(E161) (E160/100)
```

The worksheet needs the ability to accept input from users so that it can model "what if?" situations. However, a fixed set of starting values must always be present, so that the worksheet always begins with the data it was originally created with and so that users can restore the worksheet to its "default" values whenever necessary. In this case, this is achieved by creating a second set of starting values that users will be unable to alter.

In order to create the second set of starting values, copy the block A150..F161 to A200. Alter the values and formulas in this new section so that they appear as shown:

```
STARTING VALUES FOR MEGAWIDGET CASHFLOW FORECAST
________________________________________________

SELLING PRICE        10.05 £
STARTING SALES        1100 UNITS
SALES GROWTH P.M.        5 % GIVING    0.05
MATERIALS COST P.U.   5.75 £
LABOUR COST P.U.      1.23 £
POWER COST P.U.       0.77 £
MONTHLY RENTAL        3000 £
SAVINGS ACCOUNT      25000 £
INTEREST RATE P.A. 12 % - OR 1 % PER MONTH - GIVING  0.01
```

```
(C202) 9.99
(C203) 1000
(C204) 5
(C205) 5.75
(C206) 1.23
(C207) 0.77
(C208) 3000
(C209) 25000
(C210) 12
(E204)  (C204/100)
(E210)  (C210/12)
(E211)  (E210/100)
```

7.6 Monte Carlo Analysis

Simulating the effect of "chance" can help managers and other professionals to judge the risks involved in taking any particular course of action. However, merely adding a set of random numbers to a worksheet will do nothing more than confuse everyone involved. More seriously, it might even disguise potentially dangerous sets of circumstances. The major disadvantages of introducing random factors without a set of logical rules are:

* The experience of management staff is ignored

* Historical factors are ignored. For example, assuming that over the past 10 years, demand has grown by an average of 5% per month, a prediction of a 100% growth in demand would be both unprecendented and unrealistic.

* "Common sense" judgement is ignored. For example, how likely is it that demand will drop to 0 overnight?

A better way of allowing for random events is by creating a list of possible outcomes and basing calculations upon the likelihood of any given outcome.

For example, MegaWidget International expects sales to grow by an average of 5% per month. It would be extremely unlikely for sales growth to exceed 10% in any one month. Asked to weigh up the chances of sales growths between 0% and 10%, the company's sales manager produces the following table:

Sales Growth	Probability	Cumulative Value (%)
0	5	5
1	5	10
2	5	15
3	10	25
4	10	35
5	30	65
6	10	75
7	10	85
8	5	90
9	5	95
10	5	100

Working through the table, we can see that the sales manager assigns a 5% chance of a 0% sales growth, a 5% chance of a 1% sales growth and so on. Of course, the sales manager has based his table upon his previous experience in the company, his knowledge of the market and a variety of other factors.

Assured of the sales manager's competence, we could now use these figures as a reference or look up table in the worksheet. Since we are dealing with percentages, we could generate one or more random numbers between 1 and 100 and then see where they lie in the table:

Random Number	Sales Growth
6	1
42	5
17	3
87	8
29	4
63	5
51	5
4	0
72	6
38	5

Thus, in MegaWidget's cashflow forecast, figures generated as shown below could be substituted for the fixed 5% growth presently assumed.

Using this method, a random element can be introduced into the worksheet since it is controlled by a logical and reasonable set of rules. However, the accuracy of the method can be improved further still by averaging the results of the worksheet over a number of recalculations. For example, at present a freak occurrence might predict an average annual sales growth of 10% or no growth at all. Since our sales manager is confident of a 5% growth, this would clearly be at odds with his judgement and experience. By recalculating the worksheet hundreds or even thousands of times, we can produce an average figure that can be relied upon more easily.

We can reduce this technique to four basic steps:

* Decide on the possible outcomes you want to account for in the analysis

* Assign a probability to each outcome

* Generate a random number that can be related to the table or list of outcomes

* Recalculate the worksheet as many times as possible and average the results of the calculation

In the example given, an alternative might have been to apply a random number to the total sales for the year. However, there are a number of good reasons why this should be avoided. Firstly, this kind of technique would mean that users would know only if the company achieved a profit at the end of the year. For example, the company might generate negative monthly figures for eleven months of the year but suddenly leap into profit with huge Christmas sales. Clearly, eleven months of non-profitability might mean that the company might not exist by December! Locating potential problems on a monthly basis would allow the company to take corrective action before these problems occurred.

The second disadvantage of this technique lies in the use of only one random number to alter the total. A "freak" number, too low or too high, would significantly affect the accuracy of the worksheet. Over, say, a 100 recalculations, the effect of an abnormal random value would be reduced significantly since the more recalculations used, the more "fair" the result. Thus, it should follow that using more random numbers over the same number of recalculations allows greater scope for the worksheet to compensate for unusual random values.

A final disadvantage of this technique is simply that it reduces the level of control that the user has over the worksheet. In our example above, by February it would be relatively simple for a user to enter the actual sales figures for January and then recalculate the worksheet. As the year passed, more real figures could be entered and the accuracy of any predictions made with the worksheet would be significantly improved. Thus, using more random variables creates an "open" design that is more flexible and easier to alter.

7.7 Applying random factors to sales growth in the cashflow forecast.

In this area of the worksheet, two small tables will be created in order to add a random element to the figure used for monthly sales growth. The first table is known as a "look up table". This contains a list of possible outcomes together with a set of figures that describe the likelihood of each outcome coming about.

Create the look up table as follows. Enter the following labels:

(A100) "Look Up Table". Underline this with a row of equality signs at A101 (use "\-").
(A104) "Number"
(A106) "Prob."
(A107) "Rate"

* Working across from B104, enter the numbers from 1 to 10, ending at K104 (these are labels).

* Fill A103 with a row of minus signs (use "\-"). Copy this across the range B103..K103. Repeat this for A105 and the range B105..K105.

* Fill A108 with a row of minus signs (use "\-"). Copy this across the range B108..K108.

Enter the following numbers:

(B106) 0
(B107) 0.5
(C106) 5
(C107) 1
(D106) 10
(D107) 1.5
(E106) 25
(E107) 2
(F106) 45
(F107) 3
(G106) 60
(G107) 4
(H106) 75
(H107) 5
(I106) 80

```
(I107) 5.5
(J106) 85
(J107) 6
(K106) 90
(K107) 6.5
```

The second table determines which of the ten possible amounts will be added to each monthly sales growth figure.

Create the second table as follows. Enter the following labels:

(A110) "Sales Growth". Underline this with a row of equality signs at A111 (use "\-").
(A113) "Month"
(A115) "Rand."
(A117) "Growth"

* Starting at B114 and working across, enter the names of the months, ending with "Dec" at M113.

* Fill A114 with a row of minus signs (use "\-"). Copy this across the range B114..M114. Repeat this for A116 and the range B116..M116.

* Fill A118 with a row of minus signs (use "\-"). Copy this across the range B118..M118.

Enter the following formulas:

```
(B115) @INT(@RAND*100)+1
(B117) @HTABLE((B115),$B$106..$K$107,1)
```

* Copy the formula at B115 across the range C115..M115.

* Copy the formula at B117 across the range C117..M117.

You can now take a little time to see how this technique actually works. The formulas in the "Rand" row generate a set of random numbers. Each formula in the "Growth" row searches the look up table for the value closest to the random number in the corresponding "Rand" column. When the closest match is found, it takes the value stored in the "Rate" column and returns it to the "Growth" row.

It may help to make things a little clearer if we take a more concrete example:

LOOK UP TABLE
============

NO.	1	2	3	4	5
PROB	0	5	10	25	45
RATE	0.5	1	1.5	2	3

SALES GROWTH
===========

MONTH	JAN	FEB
RAND.	13	16
GROWTH	1.5	1.5

For January, a random number of 13 is produced (in the "Rand" row). The @HTABLE function in the "Growth" row searches the "Prob" row in the look up table and finds that the closest match to 13 occurs between numbers 3 and 4 (10% - 25%). In the "Rate" row below number 3 is the value 1.5. Thus, the @HTABLE function returns a value of 1.5%. In other words, in this case, the random number 13 generates a value of 1.5% to be added to the figure used to calculate the monthly sales growth for January.

Press F9 (Recalc) a few times and observe how the figures in the second table change. Match up the random numbers that are generated with their positions in the look up table. You should see that the growth figures returned match the position of each random number in the look up table.

7.8 Creating the cashflow forecast area

Now that most of the information needed by the worksheet is present, we can construct the cashflow forecast area. Enter the following labels:

(AA1) "MegaWidget International - Cashflow Forecast". Underline this with a row of equality signs (use "\-") at AA2.
(AA11) "Subtotal".
(AA14) "Cash Outflows". Underline this with a row of minus signs at AA15.
(AA16) "Materials"
(AA17) "Labour"
(AA18) "Power, Heat, Light"
(AA19) "Premises"
(AA21) "Subtotal"
(AA25) "Monthly Balance"
(AA5) "Cash Inflows". Underline this with a row of minus signs at AA6.
(AA7) "Sales (Units)"
(AA8) "Sales (£)"
(AA9) "Interest".

* Enter a row of minus signs at AA12 and copy this across the range AB12..AN12.

* Starting from AC3, enter the names of the months, ending with December at AN3. Underline these with equality signs (using "\-"), beginning from AC4.

* At AA10 enter a row of minus signs (using "\-") and copy this across the range AB10..AN10.

* Enter a row of minus signs at AA20 and copy this across the range AB20..AN20. Do the same for AA22 and the range AB22..AN22.

* Enter a row of equality signs at AA24. Copy this across the range AB24..AN24. Do the same for AA26 and the range AB26..AN26.

Now enter the following formulas:

(AC7) +C153

(AC8) (AC7*$C$152) Copy this formula across the range AD8..AN8.

(AC9) `($E$161*$C$159)` Copy this formula across the range AD9..AN9.

(AC11) `@SUM(AC8..AC9)` Copy this formula across the range AD11..AN11.

(AC16) `(AC7*$C$155)` Copy this formula across the range AD16..AN16.

(AC17) `(AC7*$C$156)` Copy this formula across the range AD17..AN17.

(AC18) `(AC7*$C$157)` Copy this formula across the range AD18..AN18.

(AC19) `+$C$158` Copy this formula across the range AD19..AN19.

(AC21) `@SUM(AC16..AC19)` Copy this formula across the range AD21..AN21.

(AC25) `(AC11-AC21)`

(AD7) `(AC7*(1+(C117/100)))` Copy this formula across the range AE7..AN7.

(AD25) `(AC25+AD11-AD21)` Copy this formula across the range AE25..AN25.

(AP7) `@SUM(AC7..AN7)` Copy this formula across the range AP8..AP9.

(AP11) `@SUM(AC11..AN11)`

(AP16) `@SUM(AC16..AN16)` Copy this formula across the range P17.AP19.

(AP21) `@SUM(AC21..AN21)`

Format this section of the worksheet so that all of the numbers are displayed properly. Pay particular attention that monetary values are displayed as currencies and that labels can be read easily. Note that any figures seen will be incorrect since there are still several more sections that need to be added to the worksheet before it will function properly.

	JAN	FEB	MARCH	APRIL
CASH INFLOWS				
SALES (UNITS)		0	0	0
SALES (£)	£0.00	£0.00	£0.00	£0.00
INTEREST	£0.00	£0.00	£0.00	£0.00
SUBTOTAL	£0.00	£0.00	£0.00	£0.00
CASH OUTFLOWS				
MATERIALS	£0.00	£0.00	£0.00	£0.00
LABOUR	£0.00	£0.00	£0.00	£0.00
POWER, LIGHT, HEAT	£0.00	£0.00	£0.00	£0.00
PREMISES	£3,000.00	£3,000.00	£3,000.00	£3,000.00
SUBTOTAL	£3,000.00	£3,000.00	£3,000.00	£3,000.00
MONTHLY BALANCE	(£3,000.00)	(£6,000.00)	(£9,000.00)	(£12,000.00)

7.9 Data entry screens

The data entry screen is an extremely important part of the worksheet. From the spreadsheet designer's point of view, it can be used in the development process to test new sections of the worksheet as they are created and is another way of testing the integrity of the model as a whole. In terms of decision support (see 7.2), it is essential that the worksheet is as simple as possible to control. One of the major design requirements of any worksheet is that it should allow the user to concentrate on the information provided by the model rather than on the mechanics of the spreadsheet program itself. In computing jargon, this is generally known as creating a *transparent application.*

In the example worksheet the major advantages of adding a data entry screen are:

* it allows managers to model complex situations with little or no technical knowledge

* it displays statistics and other information derived from the worksheet in a single location and in an appropriate form

* it allows a printed report to be produced quickly and easily

* it reduces the time taken to construct different models

* it is intuitive in that the instructions, functions and facilities likely to be needed by the user have been anticipated and provided for. Two ways in which this has been achieved have been by adding macros to store results and restore default settings.

7.10 Creating the example data entry screen

To create a basic data entry screen in the current worksheet, enter the following labels:

(BD1) "Data Entry Screen". Underline this with a row of equality signs (use "\-") at BD2.
(BA3) "Selling Price:"
(BA4) "Starting Sales:"
(BA5) "Materials Cost:"
(BA6) "Labour Cost:"
(BA7) "Power Cost:"
(BA8) "Investment:"
(BA9) "Interest Rate:"
(BA13) "Total Sales (Units):"
(BA14) "Total Sales (£):"
(BA15) "Total Expenses:"
(BA16) "E.O.Y. Balance:"
(BF3) "Average E.O.Y."
(BF4) "Balance"

At BA11 enter a line of minus signs (use "\-"). Copy this across the range BB11..BF11. Repeat this for BA17 and the range BB17..BF17.

In a little while, some macros will be created for a variety of functions, including storing results and averaging calculations. Anticipating this, add these extra labels:

(BA18) "Press ALT-R to restore default data"
(BA19) "Press ALT-A for average over 100 calculations"

```
(BA20) "Press ALT-S to store results"
```

Enter the following numbers and formulas. Note that the values for BD3..BD9 are not essential. These have been added for the sake of completeness and to allow you to format the relevant cells to display values as currencies.

```
(BD3)  9.99
(BD4)  1000
(BD5)  5.75
(BD6)  1.23
(BD7)  0.77
(BD8)  25000
(BD9)  12
(BF13)  +AP7
(BF14)  +AP8
(BF15)  +AP21
(BF16)  +AN25
```

```
              DATA ENTRY SCREEN
                                   ================
   SELLING PRICE:                          £9.99        AVERAGE E.O.Y.
   STARTING SALES:                          1000           BALANCE
   MATERIALS COST:                         £5.75
   LABOUR COST:                            £1.23
   POWER COST:                             £0.77
   INVESTMENT:                        £25,000.00
   INTEREST RATE:                          12.00
  ______________________________
  TOTAL SALES (UNITS):                                     14111
  TOTAL SALES (£):                                   £140,968.18
  TOTAL EXPENSES:                                    £145,359.70
  E.O.Y. BALANCE:                                    (£1,391.52)
  ______________________________
  Press ALT-R to restore default data
  Press ALT-A for average over 100 calculations
  Press ALT-S to save results
```

7.11 Adding macros

It is now time to add macros to the worksheet, to automate some of the more tedious processes and to make overall operation a little simpler for the end-user.

The first set of macros simply allow the user to move around the worksheet quickly and efficiently. Enter the macro data and their accompanying labels into the worksheet at the co-ordinates given. Remember that the macros will only work when they have been named (see 6.14 - 6.16). To create a macro name, use the command sequence "/RNC". When asked to enter a name, use "\" to represent the ALT key, followed by the macro letter. For example, the first macro's name would be entered as "\M".

```
(A53) {GOTO A100}~
(C53) "ALT-M GO TO MONTE CARLO DATA"

(A55) {GOTO AA1}~
(C55) "ALT-C GO TO CASHFLOW FORECAST"

(A57) {GOTO A150}~
(C57) "ALT-D GO TO DEFAULT DATA"

(A59) {GOTO A50}~
(C59) "ALT-K GO TO MACROS"

(A61) {GOTO BA1}~
(C61) "ALT-E GO TO DATA ENTRY SCREEN"

(G53) {GOTO CA1}~
(I53) "ALT-P GO TO REPORT AREA"
```

Note that the tilde ("~") represents the Enter key.

The next macro seems a little more complex but relies entirely upon a single command for its operation. As you will see from the title, the purpose of the macro is to restore the default settings of the data entry screen. This will allow users to rectify mistakes when modelling without having to manually re-enter the default data each time.

The "LET" command is similar to the LET statement in BASIC. It assigns a value, formula or string to a given cell regardless of the user's current position in the worksheet. In this macro, information is copied from the starting values area of the worksheet into corresponding positions in the data entry screen. Enter the data as shown and name the range as described earlier.

```
(C63) "ALT-R RESTORE DEFAULT VALUES"
```

```
(A63)  {LET BD3,+C202}~
(A64)  {LET BD4,+C203}~
(A65)  {LET BD5,+C205}~
(A66)  {LET BD6,+C206}~
(A67)  {LET BD7,+C207}~
(A68)  {LET BD8,+C209}~
(A69)  {LET BD9,+C210}~
```

The next macro becomes more complex still. The purpose of this sequence is to average the company's end-of-year balance over a 100 recalculations. As explained earlier, this helps to offset the effects of any freak conditions created by using Monte Carlo Analysis (see 7.6) and provides a firmer result upon which to base decisions. For the moment, enter the macro data as shown. An explanation of how the macro works follows.

```
(A71)  "ALT-A AVERAGE BALANCE (100 CALCS)"
(E72)  "COUNTER"
(E73)  "CUMULATIVE TOTAL"
(E74)  "AVERAGE"

(A73)  {LET D72,+0}~
(A74)  {LET D73,+0}~
(A75)  {BLANK BF6..BF6}~
(A76)  {IF D72=101}{JUMP A83}~
(A77)  {CALC}~
(A78)  {LET D72,D72+1}~
(A79)  {LET D73,D73+AN25}~
(A80)  {LET BF7,'*COUNTING*}~
(A81)  {LET BF8,D72}~
(A82)  {JUMP A76}~
(A83)  {BLANK BF7..BF8}~
(A84)  {LET BF6,D73/100}~
```

The first step we must take is to create a counter that will keep a record of the number of recalculations made by the spreadsheet. The cell we will use for this is located at D72. Each time the macro is used, we must reset the counter to zero. This is performed by the line at A73.

```
(A73)  {LET D72,+0}~
```

We can cause the spreadsheet to carry out the same actions a number of times by using a LOOP. In this macro, the loop works by "jumping" to different locations in the macro according to the results of a test. The diagram below might help to make things clearer.

```
1. Start of loop...

2.  Test - if positive go to (5), otherwise carry on with (3)

3. Actions...

4. Go back to the start of the loop at (1)

5. Actions...
```

For our counter, the sequence of logic appears thus:

```
1. Start of loop

2. Test: has the counter reached 100? If so, go to (6),
   otherwise carry on with (3)

3. Add 1 to the counter

4. Other actions...

5. Go back to the start of the loop at (1)

6. The action has been carried out 100 times...
```

As you can see, if the counter has not yet reached 100, the actions at (3) and (4) will be carried out. As soon as the counter reaches 100, the routine "jumps" to (6). Of course, one of the "other actions" in (4) will be the command to recalculate the worksheet. In this way, the worksheet will be recalculated exactly 100 times.

If we use the simple labels given above, the structure of the macro should now become much clearer:

```
(A76) {IF D72=101}{JUMP A83}~
     Start of loop: if the counter goes above 100, go to A83
(A77) {CALC}~
```

```
        Recalculate the worksheet

    (A78) {LET D72,D72+1}~
        Add 1 to the counter
    (A79)
    (A80)
    (A81)
    (A82) {JUMP A76}~
        Go back to the start of the loop at A76
    (A83) {BLANK BF7..BF8}~
        The actions have been carried out 100 times,continue from
        this point
```

Thus, the creation of a loop structure allows us to specifiy how many times a set of actions will be performed.

The "JUMP" command instructs the macro to move to the specified location and continue from that point.

So that we can calculate the average balance over 100 calculations, we need to keep a cumulative total. This is done by recalculating the worksheet and then adding the end-oy-year balance to the contents of D73. Once again, we must reset the cumulative total to zero each time the macro is used. This is done by the line at A74.

```
(A74) {LET D73,+0}~
```

The command at A79 is placed within the loop to give the sum of 100 new end-of-year balance figures.

```
(A79) {LET D73,D73+AN25}~
```

It should be remembered that causing the worksheet to be recalculated 100 times may involve a quite lengthy wait (depending on the speed of the computer being used). After waiting two or three minutes for something to happen, it would be understandable if a user panicked with the thought that the machine had crashed. With this in mind, it might be helpful to give users a progress report, so that they can see what is happening at any given time. We can do this by utilising the contents of the cell we have designated as a counter together with an appropriate message.

The line at A75 uses the "BLANK" command to erase the contents of BF6. This is the cell that will be used to hold the average end-of-year balance obtained at the end of the macro. We will erase the contents of this cell each time the macro is run to avoid any possible confusion on the part of the user.

```
(A75) {BLANK BF6..BF6}~
```

As the loop is repeated, the counter is increased by one each time. We can use this to our advantage and create a "countdown" message on the data entry screen. Once again, we place these commands in the loop so that are repeated each time the counter is altered.

```
(A80) {LET BF7,'*COUNTING*}~ (A81) {LET BF8,D72}~
```

When the loop ends, we must erase the message on the screen. This is done by using the "BLANK" command once more.

```
(A83) {BLANK BF7..BF8}~
```

Finally, we divide the sum of the end-of-year balances by 100 to give and average figure and place this in the data entry screen at BF6.

```
(A84) {LET BF6,D73/100}~
```

Having gained an insight into the overall structure and logic of the macro, we can now examine the listing again:

```
(A73) {LET D72,+0}~
    Set the counter cell to zero

(A74) {LET  D73,+0}~
    Set  the  cumulative  total cell to zero

(A75) {BLANK BF6..BF6}~
    Erase any previous cumulative total display

(A76)  {IF D72=101}{JUMP  A83}~
    Begin the loop with a test. If the counter exceeds 100, go to
    A83

(A77) {CALC}~
    Recalculate the worksheet
```

```
(A78) {LET D72,D72+1}~
    Add 1 to the counter

(A79) {LET D73,D73+AN25}~
    Add the end-of-year balance to the cumulative total

(A80) {LET BF7,'*COUNTING*}~
    Display a message to the user

(A81) {LET BF8,D72}~
    Display the value of the counter cell as a "countdown
    marker"

(A82) {JUMP A76}~
    Return to the start of the loop

(A83) {BLANK BF7..BF8}~
    Erase the message to the  user

(A84) {LET BF6,D73/100}~
    Place the average end-of-year balance
```

At first glance, the command at A80 need not be performed 100 times, particularly since it slows down the execution of the macro. Normally, the message would be displayed prior to the start of the loop and then deleted at the end of the macro. However, repeating the command causes a flickering effect that could be used to draw attention to the text of the message.

The use of GOTO and JUMP commands is frowned upon by programmers since it encourages linear (as opposed to structured) programming. In later versions of AsEasyAs and other packages, the need to use this kind of technique is removed entirely by the inclusion of a FOR..NEXT construct. The FOR..NEXT command takes the following structure:

```
FOR X Repetitions

Actions...

NEXT X
```

This approach offers three major advantages over the JUMP command:

* it forms a self-contained routine

* it avoids the need to specify absolute coordinates

* it simplifies the structure of the macro

7.12 Creating a report area

Before looking at the report macros, we must first reserve an area in the worksheet for the report. Enter the following labels:

```
(CA1)  "Report Area".
```
Underline this with a row of equality signs in CA2 (use '\=").

```
(CA4)  "Starting"
(CA5)  "Sales"
(CB4)  "Selling"
(CB5)  "Price"
(CC4)  "Materials"
(CD4)  "Labour"
(CE4)  "Power"
(CF4)  "Investment"
(CG4)  "Interest"
(CG5)  "Rate"
(CH4)  "Total"
(CH5)  "Sales (£)"
(CI4)  "Total"
(CI5)  "Expenses"
(CJ4)  "E.O.Y."
(CJ5)  "Balance"
(CK4)  "Average"
(CK5)  "E.O.Y. Balance"
(BZ20) "Use ALT-S to store results"
```

* Starting from BZ7 and working downwards, enter labels from "1." to "12.". Remember that these are labels and will need to be prefixed with a single quote (').

* Fill CA6 with a row of minus signs (use "\-"). Copy this across the range CB6..CK6.

* Fill BZ19 with a row of minus signs (use "\-"). Copy this across the range CA19..CK19.

Our last two macros are used to create report detail lines in the worksheet that store sets of data that are of interest to the user. For example, a user might discover a set of circumstances that might cause a substantial improvement in the company's profits. Rather than take the time and trouble to write down the information on a piece of paper (which may become lost), this can be stored within the worksheet itself. In this way, the user can find 10, 20 or even more solutions to a problem, store them all automatically within the worksheet and then print a final report via the program's printing facilities. Although the example that follows is relatively unsophisticated, it demonstrates this concept admirably.

When designing the macro, a major consideration must be how to treat any existing reports when the worksheet is loaded by another user. The most sensible answer need not cause any headaches: simply give each user their own copy of the worksheet on a disk.

Assuming that only one person will be using the example worksheet, a compromise must be found between retaining important information generated during previous sessions and making room for new entries. In this example macro, a reasonable solution has been reached by manipulating the way it is constructed.

The macro operates by "filling in" a simple table in a reserved area of the worksheet. Briefly, each entry is made according to the following instructions:

* move to the top left hand corner of the table

* move downwards a set number of rows, according to the value of a counter

* copy the data horizontally across the table, fixing it so that further recalculations of the worksheet will not cause it to alter

* increment the counter

I our case, the only modification we need make to this set of rules is to specify that the counter should be reset to the starting position of the table each time the worksheet is loaded. This will mean that new report lines will overwrite any previous lines that were stored when the worksheet was last saved. The advantage of this is that the "old" report information is retained for as long as possible since it is only erased a little at a time - and only when a new set of data is placed into the report.

If the counter is located at J56, the first of our two macros must be an AUTOEXEC macro. An AUTOEXEC macro is one that is executed automatically each time the worksheet is loaded. The program identifies which macro to run by its unique name: 0 (zero). The macro below assigns a value of zero to J56 each time the worksheet is loaded.

```
(A86) "AUTOEXEC MACRO (SETS COUNTER TO ZERO FOR REPORT AREA)"
(A87) {LET J56,+0}~
```

Remember to name the macro "\0".

Having established a default value for our position counter, we can now create the second macro. Once again, although the macro appears to be extremely complex, it does little more than access the program's menu system to carry out basic copying operations. Begin by entering the following labels:

```
(K56) "COUNTER 1"
(K57) "TOTAL SALES"
(K58) "TOTAL EXPENSES"
(K59) "E.O.Y BALANCE"
(K60) "COUNTER 2"
(G55) "ALT-S CREATE A REPORT AREA AND STORE VALUES"
```

Now enter the macro instructions as listed below. Note that some commands are followed by two tildes ("~"), which represent the Enter key being pressed twice.

```
(G56) {GOTO CA6}~
(G57) {LET J56,J56+1}~
(G58) {LET J60,+0}~
(G59) {LET J60,J60+1}~
(G60) {DN}~
(G61) {IF J60<J56}{JUMP G59}~
(G62) /RCVBD4~~
(G63) {RT}~
(G64) /RCVBD3~~
(G65) {RT}~
(G66) /RCVBD5~~
(G67) {RT}~
(G68) /RCVBD6~~
(G69) {RT}~
```

```
(G70) /RCVBD7~~
(G71) {RT}~
(G72) /RCVBD8~~
(G73) {RT}~
(G74) /RCVBD9~~
(G75) {RT}~
(G76) /RCVBF14~~
(G77) {RT}~
(G78) /RCVBF15~~
(G79) {RT}~
(G80) /RCVBF16~~
(G81) {RT}~
(G82) /RCVBF6~~
```

The first command moves us to a suitable starting position in the table, ready to begin moving values into the report area.

```
(G56) {GOTO CA6}~
```

The next command simply adds 1 to the value of the position counter.

```
(G57) {LET J56,J56+1}~
```

In order to move around the table, we will need to compare the value of the position counter against a second "working" counter. The second counter is located at J60 and the next two commands ensure that its initial value is set to zero before adding 1 to it.

```
(G58) {LET J60,+0}~
(G59) {LET J60,J60+1}~
```

The command at G56 moved the current cell position to the row above the first entry in the table. A {DN} command now places us at the very first entry in the report.

```
(G60) {DN}~
```

Now we come to the most complex part of the routine - the loop that moves the cursor to the correct position in the report. Although it is not immediately apparent, when the commands at G59 and G60 are used in conjunction with an {IF} command, they create a simple loop that moves the cursor downwards until it is in the correct position in the report. Look at the commands in combination:

```
(G59) {LET J60,J60+1}~ (G60) {DN}~ (G61) {IF J60<J56}{JUMP G59}~
```

The logic of this sequence can be shown as a list of steps to be performed until a specified condition is fulfilled.

1. Add 1 to the "working" counter (Counter 2)

2. Move the cursor down by one row

3. Compare Counter 2 with the position counter (Counter 1). If it is less than the position counter, go back to (1).

The position counter tells us how many entries there are in the table. Each time the macro is executed, the position counter is incremented by 1.Thus, if the macro has been used 10 times, the position counter will be set at 10, meaning that we must move down that number of rows in the table to add a new entry. If Counter 2 is less than the position counter, we have not moved far enough down. If that happens, we move down one more row and carry out the test again. The process of moving down and testing the counters continues until we are in the correct position in the table.

All of the remaining commands are paired and perform the same basic copying function. The first command in each pair activates the program's menu system and copies a cell to the current position as a VALUE. Copying using the value option means that the data will remain fixed - as if entered manually as a number or label. If the data were to be copied in the normal way, any recalculation of the worksheet would change it in the table. After copying information to the current cell position, the {RT} command moves us to the next position in the table, ready to copy another piece of information.

```
(G62) /RCVBD4~~
(G63) {RT}~
```

There is no mystery as to the contents of the cells that carry out the copying procedures. Each sequence of characters corresponds to a sequence of keystrokes. Let's take the contents of G62 as an example:

/ Activate the main menu.

R Activate the "Range" sub-menu.

C Select "Copy".
V Select "Value".

BD4 Mark BD4 as the start of the block to be copied.

~ Press Enter to also mark BD4 as the end of the block to be copied.

~ Press Enter again to accept the current cell position as the destination for the copied data.

Although the report section of the worksheet is functional, it does lack a number of refinements. There are several ways in which it could be improved.

At present, there are 12 "spaces" in the table for entries. No check is made to see if the position counter exceeds 12, meaning that more than 12 entries can be made. If this happens, new detail lines will not be numbered and will erase the text at the bottom of the table. This can be rectified by using an {IF} command to check the value of the position counter. If the counter exceeds 12, an error message can be displayed and execution of the macro can be halted.

A new macro could be created to add automatic saving. This would remove any need for the user to access the command menus, specify file names etc.

A new macro could be created to send the report to the printer automatically. With a little ingenuity, it would also be possible to test when the current table had been filled, send this data to the printer, erase the contents of the table and then reset the position counter to 1. In effect, this would give users a permanent progress report of their modelling activities and would ensure that the table was always kept to a manageable size.

Where the worksheet is restricted to a certain size, there is the danger that the report might exceed the program's capabilities. It would be wise to add a checking routine that detected when the user had reached the bottom of the worksheet. Again, an {IF} statement with an accompanying error message could be used.

7.13 Tidying up the example worksheet

Before moving on to some new techniques, take some time to review the the presentation of the worksheet and to make alterations where needed.

Begin by examining all of the labels used in the worksheet. Ensure that they meet the following guidelines:

* each section of the worksheet should be named in such a way that the purpose of the section is made clear

* where necessary, labels should be added as comments, to clarify any areas that might cause confusion

* units should be given where possible

* instructions on how to operate any of the worksheet's features should be given

For more information on labels and titles, see sections 4.4 and 4.5.

The next step is to make sure that all of the columns in the worksheet display number and currencies in the correct format. Work through the model and change cell formats and column widths as necessary (see 4.9 amd 4.11). Remember, unless the column width is set to a large enough value, some numbers may not be displayed properly, being shown as a row of asterisks instead.

```
MEGAWIDGET INTERNATIONAL - CASHFLOW FORECAST
==============================================

This model represents the cashflow forecast for MegaWidget International
for the period January 1993 - December 1993.

This model constructed by Paul Bocij, Director of Financial Planning

The cashflow forecast is stored at AA1 (ALT-C)
The macro data is stored at A50 (ALT-K)
The default data is stored at A150 (ALT-D)*   See Note
The Monte Carlo Analysis data is stored at A100 (ALT-M)
The results screen is stored at BA1 (ALT-E)
The report area is located at CA1 (ALT-P)
```

An introductory screen has not yet been added to the worksheet. Look back at sections 5.4 and 5.18 and create an introductory screen for this worksheet. Remember to include a title, your name, basic instructions, the locations of the main sections of the worksheet and macro key assignments. A sample introductory screen is shown below:

At this point, it is wise to test the accuracy of the worksheet by comparing the program's output against a set of figures calculated manually. If the worksheet works correctly, at least two copies of it should be saved to disk. You can now delete some of the older versions of the worksheet from the disk, although you should keep enough files to retain a "history" of the project.

Imagine that you have saved the worksheet at regular intervals during its development. Keeping copies of these files serve two very important purposes:

* if all copies of the final version of the worksheet are lost or destroyed, it can be reconstructed quickly from the earlier versions of the model

* if an entirely new model needs to be constructed, these files might reduce the amount of work involved since they are likely to contain sections that can be copied into the new worksheet

7.14 Protecting cells

It is possible to protect ranges of cells so that their contents can not be altered accidentally. This can be useful on a variety of occasions, for example in data entry screens.

To mark a range of cells as "locked" (unable to be altered), use the following procedure:

* Press "/" to access the main menu

* From the main menu, press "W" or the Enter key to access the "Worksheet" sub-menu

* From the Worksheet sub-menu, press "G" to access the "General" sub-menu

* From the "General" sub-menu, press "P" to access the "Protect" sub-menu

* Select "Enable" to switch on the protection feature

The keystroke sequence for the above operation is "/WGPE". When the protection feature is enabled, it will be necessary to mark various ranges of cells to inform the program whether or not they can be altered.

* Press "/" to access the main menu

* Press "R" to access the "Range" sub-menu

* From the Range sub-menu, select "Lock"

* Select "Yes" to prevent alterations to a range or "No" to allow the range to be modified

* Mark the range of cells in the normal way (see 4.10)

The keystroke sequence for this operation is "/RLY" or "/RLN".

7.15 Protecting cells in the data entry screen

As mentioned in the previous section, it can often be useful to prevent users from accidentally making changes to sections of the worksheet. In the case of the data entry screen, there may be items of data that should not be altered and are only present for the purposes of information. Alternatively, users might accidentally enter data into a cell containing a label.

In the case of our sample worksheet, users will not be permitted to alter any cells other than those in the data entry screen. This will make the model more secure in that starting values and other important data will not be changed in any way.

* Enter the main menu and select "Worksheet"

* Select "General" and then choose "Protect"

* Select "Enable" to set the worksheet so that no cells can be altered

* Move to the data entry screen (use our Alt-E macro) and then activate the "Range" sub-menu ("/R")

* Select "Lock", followed by "No"

* Mark the range BD3..BD9

The keystroke sequence required for this operation is "/WGPE/RLN".

In this way, users will now be unable to alter any of the cells in the worksheet, apart from the values we have allowed them to change in the data entry screen. Whilst this may seem restrictive, it is not so: users can continue to view the worksheet, carry out recalculations, store results in the report table and manipulate the data entry screen.

7.16 Putting finishing touches to the example worksheet

For the sake of completeness, it is worth carrying out two more final procedures. The first is to generate a set of graphs that can be activated using the F10 key or the "Name" sub-menu. Since the worksheet is close to that created in the previous exercise, use section 6.17 to create two sample graphs. Remember that the range co-ordinates given in the last section will need to be changed to reflect the new position of our cashflow forecast in the worksheet.

The final change needed is the addition of a set of user notes describing explaining a number of important points regarding the construction of this worksheet:

* add a note to both of the starting values sections, explaining that two copies exist because the worksheet was developed from an earlier exercise. Remember to mention that one set contains a permanent set of starting values whilst the other is altered by entries made in the data entry screen.

* document all of the macros, noting important cells such as those that begin loops and those that use counters.

* add a note to the report section of the worksheet, explaining that selecting "Go" from the Print sub- menu will output the report - not the whole of the worksheet - to the printer. Remember to set the range for printing so that this will actually happen!

* where applicable, add notes in the different section of the worksheet to tell users which macros are available for use. For example, in the report area, add lines to describe the Alt-S and Alt-R macros.

The worksheet is now completed and can be saved to disk under its final name.

7.17 Summary

In this section you have learned how to:

* Account for random factors in a worksheet

* Understand advanced concepts: Monte Carlo Analysis, Competitive Advantage, Decision Support Systems, look-up tables, loops, transparent applications

* Restore an altered worksheet to its default settings

* Copy absolute values

* Generate automatic tables and reports

* Create complex macros

* Protect cells from accidental alteration

Section 8: Database And Advanced Functions

8.1 Objective

This section demonstrates some of the more advanced functions found in modern spreadsheet packages. Recent developments in spreadsheet design have allowed programs to incorporate a number of powerful new features. Chief amongst these are database functions and three-dimensional worksheets. Although a complete treatment of these areas would be impractical, the aim of this section is to familiarise users with the use of these techniques.

8.2 What is a database?

The term "database" is often used inaccurately. It is important that users distinguish between a database *program* and a database *file*.

Traditionally, most people would describe a database package as a program designed to assist with the electronic storage and manipulation of information. However, such a loose definition could apply equally well to word processors, communications packages and even adventure games. It is only when we look at the traditional description of a database file that any real distinctions can be made. A database is made up fields and records as follows:

Field: A unit of information

Record: A collection of related fields

Database: a collection of related records

An example of a manual database system might be an address book. Pieces of information such as names, postal codes and telephone numbers can be considered to be fields. When all of the fields related to one person are gathered together (name, address, telephone number), they constitute a record. A collection of records - the address book - is a database.

So far, there seems very little to recommend that use of the a computerised database system over a manual one. A complete treatment of this subject is beyond the scope of this book, however here are just a few of the advantages that a computerised system holds over its manual counterpart:

* Speed - the computer can sort through millions of records in seconds. ATM (Automatic Teller Machines - or "Cashpoint") systems carry out transactions "live". When you insert your card in the machine, it reads your current balance, dispenses the money you request and records the withdrawal all within the few minutes you spend standing at the machine. Consider that the bank might have several million customers each with their own card and the sheer speed of such a system becomes apparent.

* Searching - the computer can search a database for almost any piece of data in a fraction of the time it would take a human.

* Reduction in storage requirements. A single floppy disk can store the equivalent of approximately 400 pages of text: a single filing cabinet could hold literally millions of records if they were stored on magnetic media.

* Automation - a huge number of operations can be carried out automatically, improving the speed, accuracy and efficiency of almost any activity. Good examples include payroll, mailing list and stock control operations.

It is worthwhile taking a few seconds to review the major points made in this section:

Database programs allow us to record and manipulate data electronically.

A database is a collection of information, made up of records and fields.

The main advantages of electronic database systems over manual ones are concerned with improved productivity, due to the speed and accuracy of the computer.

Many software houses suggest that their spreadsheet products combine the benefits of a spreadsheet with those of a powerful database system. These claims tend to arise from the fact that spreadsheet programs handle data in much the same way as database systems. However, a spreadsheet can not eliminate the need for dedicated database systems since these are specialised programs designed with a different set of objectives in mind. On the other hand, it is possible to take advantage of the database functions included in most spreadsheet packages to create some basic - but still extremely powerful - applications.

8.3 Using data tables

A particularly useful spreadsheet tool is the ability to create and manipulate tables of data. This first sample worksheet shows how a spreadsheet can be made to "fill in the blanks".

Imagine that we want to calculate the monthly repayments needed for a loan of £20,000 taken over a 10 year period. In selecting a lender, we need to take into account the different interest rates charged by various companies. A good way of doing this would be to calculate the monthly repayment for the loan using a range of different interest values and display the results in the form of a table. We can do this by using the spreadsheet's program built-in table functions.

A complete listing of the worksheet is given in Appendix 4. This should be used in conjunction with the notes that follow to allow you to construct the sample worksheet. As you construct the worksheet, remember to format cells to display currencies and percentages properly since this will help to make the example clearer.

The first step is to construct the basic layout of the table. Since the application is relatively small, a layout similar to that shown below is satisfactory.

Although the worksheet appears to be quite simple, a number of points need to be made about its construction.

The Data Table command requires a number of named ranges to specified before it will function correctly. In this case, the cell containing the amount of the loan (£20,000, co-ordinate B1) has been named "Principal". Similarly, the cells containing the initial interest rate (5%, co-ordinate B2) and the term of the loan (10 years, co-ordinate D1) have been named "Interest" and "Term" respectively. Refer to 4.10 for more information on how to specify and name ranges of cells.

```
        A                     B          C                   D
AMOUNT:                  £20,000.00  TERM:                  10
INTEREST RATE (PA):          5.00%  EQUATION:          £212.13


                     INTEREST RATE    PAYMENT
                     ---------  ----
                                          212.13
                              5.00%
                              5.50%
                              6.00%
******************            6.50%
* TABLE EXAMPLE 1 *           7.00%
******************            7.50%
                              8.00%
                              8.50%
                              9.00%
                              9.50%
                             10.00%
                             10.50%
```

Using the named ranges described, we can now use one of the program' built-in functions to give us an equation of:

```
@PMT(PRINCIPAL,INTEREST/12,TERM*12)
```

This equation is located in D2 and is necessary because it will be used by the Data Table command to construct the completed table. Notice how the annual interest rate is divided by 12 and the term is multiplied by 12 so that our answers will be given as monthly figures.

Since we want to work with a group of interest rates that climb in regular increments, we can take advantage of the "Fill" command to place all of these values in the worksheet for us.

* Position the cursor at the start of the column you wish to fill with values

* From the main menu, select "Data" to access the Data sub-menu

* Select "Fill"

* Highlight the range of cells you want to fill

* Enter the starting value

* Enter the value that will be used to increment each of the following cells in the marked range

The abbreviated form of this command is "/DF".

In this worksheet, we want to fill the range B8..B19 with values ranging from 5.0% to 10.5%, using an increment of 0.5%. Thus, the starting value is 0.05 and the increment value is 0.005, giving us the table shown above.

The Data Table command works by repeatedly inserting a new value into the equation and copying the results into the next position in the table until all of the "fill" values have been used. For this reason, we need to specify a location where the command can locate the data it needs to copy. We do this by copying the results of the equation into a blank cell at the top of the column we want to use for our results. In this case, we enter "+D2" (where the equation is located) at co-ordinate C7 (one cell above the start of the area we wish to use for our results).

We can now execute the Data Table command.

* From the main menu, select "Data"

* Select "Table" from the Data sub-menu

* Select "1" since we are working with only one set of variable data

* Highlight the whole of the table (B7..C19)

* Highlight B2 as the "Input Cell". Each new interest rate will be copied into B2, the equation will be evaluated and the result will be placed into the table

The abbreviated form for this sequence of key presses is "/DT1". The table should now be automatically filled in by the program and should appear as shown:

AMOUNT:	£20,000.00	TERM:		10
INTEREST RATE (PA):	5.00%	EQUATION:		£212.13
	INTEREST RATE	PAYMENT		
		£212.13		
	5.00%	£212.13		
	5.50%	£217.05		
	6.00%	£222.04		
*******************	6.50%	£227.10		
* TABLE EXAMPLE 1 *	7.00%	£232.22		
*******************	7.50%	£237.40		
	8.00%	£242.66		
	8.50%	£247.97		
	9.00%	£253.35		
	9.50%	£258.80		
	10.00%	£264.30		
	10.50%	£269.87		

What happens if we want to vary the interest rate and the term? We can do this by causing the program to deal with two sets of variable data and generating several columns for results.

Move the "+D2" from C7 to B7, so that the top of the first "results" column is clear. Now, enter 10 in C7, 15 in D7 and 20 in E7. The columns headed by these figures will now be used to store the results of the calculations using 10, 15 and 20 years as the term of the loan.

* From the main menu, select "Data"

* Select "Table" from the Data sub-menu

* Select "2" since we are now working with two sets of variable data

* Highlight the whole of the table (B7..E19)

* Highlight B2 (the interest rate) as the first "Input Cell" and D1 (the term) as the second

The abbreviated form of this command is "/DT2".

Once again, the table is filled in automatically, except that this time three columns of results are created instead of just one. The command has taken the data regarding the length of the term horizontally across C7..E7 and the data for the interest rate vertically along B8..B19. The illustration below should help to make this clearer:

AMOUNT:	£20,000.00	TERM:	10	
INTEREST RATE (PA):	5.00%	EQUATION:	£212.13	
	INTEREST RATE	PAYMENT		
	212.1310304	10	15	20
	5.00%	£212.13	£158.16	£131.99
	5.50%	£217.05	£163.42	£137.58
	6.00%	£222.04	£168.77	£143.29
******************	6.50%	£227.10	£174.22	£149.11
* TABLE EXAMPLE 1 *	7.00%	£232.22	£179.77	£155.06
******************	7.50%	£237.40	£185.40	£161.12
	8.00%	£242.66	£191.13	£167.29
	8.50%	£247.97	£196.95	£173.56
	9.00%	£253.35	£202.85	£179.95
	9.50%	£258.80	£208.84	£186.43
	10.00%	£264.30	£214.92	£193.00
	10.50%	£269.87	£221.08	£199.68

8.4 Sorting data

It can often be quite handy to be able to sort data into alphabetical or numerical order. Most spreadsheet programs contain a "Sort" command that can carry out this procedure automatically. Sorting is normally carried out by specifying a field upon which the sort will be based. For example, in address book, entries are normally stored in alphabetical order according to the surname of each person listed. The field used for sorting is normally called the *sort key*. In the case of address book, the surname field would be the sort key.

If there are a number of similar entries in a database file, it is sometimes necessary to define the way in which it will be sorted more strictly. This is usually done by having several sort keys and assigning priorities to them. Thus, it is not unusual to have a *primary sort key* and a *secondary sort key*.

The following example shows how primary and secondary sort keys operate. A database file is used to store names and addresses. Separate fields are used for initial and surname. Here are some typical (unsorted) entries in the address book:

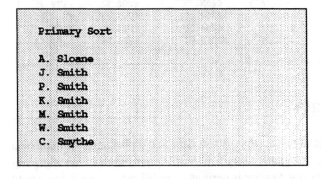

```
Unsorted Entries

J. Smith
P. Smith
K. Smith
M. Smith
W. Smith
C. Smythe
A. Sloane
```

A sorting operation is carried out using the surname field as the sort key. Since there are several people with the surname of Smith, the process is unable to distinguish between them, resulting in a new order of:

```
Primary Sort

A. Sloane
J. Smith
P. Smith
K. Smith
M. Smith
W. Smith
C. Smythe
```

Notice how only the entries concerning Sloane and Smythe have changed position in the file.

A second sorting operation is carried out using the surname as the primary sort key and the initial as the secondary sort key. The first part of the process organises the position of each entry alphabetically, according to the surname. The result at this stage is exactly the same as produced by sorting on surname alone. However, the second pass now sorts the similar entries on the basis of each person's initials. The result is quite different:

```
Primary & Secondary Sort

A. Sloane
J. Smith
K. Smith
M. Smith
P. Smith
W. Smith
C. Smythe
```

You can try this out by entering these names into the cells of a worksheet and then trying out some sort commands for yourself. First, just use a primary sort key to see how the "Smith" entries retain their original order.

* Select "Data" from the main menu to enter the Data sub-menu

* Select "Sort"

* Highlight the range of cells to be sorted

* Select the column to be used as a primary sort key (surname)

* Choose "A" for ascending order or "D" for descending order

* Select "Go" to sort the highlighted range

The abbreviated form of this command is "/DS".

Now, repeat the procedure above but specify a secondary sort column that will use each person's initials.

You should note that sorting takes place on the ASCII values of the characters in each cell. In other words, special characters (such as exclamation marks) will appear before numbers, numbers will appear before letters and capital letters before lower case letters.

8.5 Frequency distributions

Many spreadsheet programs contain the facility to construct frequency distribution tables, using the Data Bin command.

The command is used as follows:

* Enter the values to be analysed into a worksheet column

* Enter a range of bin values into a worksheet column. These figures must be in ascending order and there must be two empty columns to the right of this data (this is where the results will be filled in)

* From the main menu, select "Data"

* From the Data sub-menu, select "Bin"

* Highlight the range of cells containing the data to be analysed

* Highlight the range of cells containing the bin values

The spreadsheet will now count the values and enter the results into the two blank columns left earlier.

The following example gives a practical illustration of the use of this technique, showing how it can be applied to a variety of applications.

A quality controller wishes to construct a frequency distribution table of measurements taken from a new machine. He enters his measurements into one column of the worksheet and a set of ranges into another. The worksheet appears thus:

VALUES	BIN RANGE	COUNT	FRACTION
39	30		
40	40		
41	50		
51	60		
41	70		
38			
45			
43			
42			
41			
38			
43			
45			
41			
47			

Notice how space has been made (two blank columns) for the results of the calculation.

The calculation is performed and the results are automatically entered into the worksheet. The display now appears as shown:

VALUES	BIN RANGE	COUNT	FRACTION
39	30	0	0.00
40	40	3	0.20
41	50	11	0.73
51	60	1	0.07
41	70	0	0.00
38		0	0.00
45			
43			
42			
41			
38			
43			
45			
41			
47			

The first "count" figure describes the number of values that have fallen between 0 and 30, in this case none. The second figure shows how many values have fallen between 30 and 40 and so on.

If the quality controller's tolerances are between 40 and 60, it can be seen that machine is operating at the lower end of the range. No measurements have been taken above the specified tolerance but three have been taken below it. This may indicate a problem such as wear on the machine tool.

Although this process could have been carried out manually, the spreadsheet reduces the amount of time and labour required. Any member of staff can be used to take measurements and enter them into the worksheet. At a later point in time, the quality controller can process the measurements in a matter of seconds and diagnose potential problems. Additionally, if modifications are made to the worksheet, it can be used to keep a historical record of the machine's performance and can assist with the diagnosis of production problems.

Other applications for this command might range from analysing questionnaires to grading students' examination marks.

8.6 Goalseeking

Goalseeking involves finding the combination of factors that will produce a known or desired result. To carry out goalseeking, four values are required:

* Input - this contains a value that will be continuously amended and then inserted into a formula until the desired goal is reached

* Output - this contains the formula or expression that will be evaluated repeatedly until the desired goal is reached. The formula also defines the relationships between the cells that will be used by the goalseeking function.

* Desired - this contains the known or desired result of the calculation

* Tolerance - this dictates the accuracy of the answer; plus or minus the specified tolerance.

The goalseeking function is invoked as follows:

* From the main menu, select "Data" to enter the Data sub-menu

* Select "Goalseek" to enter the Goalskeeking sub-menu

* Specify the Input cell

* Specify the output cell (which contains the formula to be evaluated)

* Specify the known or desired result

* Specify a tolerance

The abbreviated form of this command is "/DG".

The expression will be evaluated a number of times until the desired answer is reached. Some programs generate an error message if the value can not be found at all (perhaps because an extremely small tolerance has been set) or if the answer can not be reached after a set number of calculations. The more restrictive the tolerance, the longer the program will take to reach the desired result.

Once more, a practical demonstration of goalseeking will make its value clearer.

A man requires a loan of £18,000. He has decided that he is willing to repay the loan over 10 years but that he cannot make his payments to be more than £200 per month. The current interest rate is 8.5% so the man constructs a simple worksheet to calculate what his monthly payments would be:

	A	B
1	GOALSEEKING EXAMPLE	
2	———————	
3		
4	LOAN:	£18,000.00
5	INTEREST RATE:	8.50%
6	TERM (MONTHS):	120
7	PAYMENT:	£223.17

The formula used in B7 is: @PMT(B4,B5/12,B6). Note how the interest rate is divided by 12 to obtain a monthly equivalent. Unfortunately, the worksheet shows that the man would be unable to afford the monthly payment of £223.17. However, interest rates are changing rapidly and the man realises that if he obtains a fixed-rate loan at precisely the correct moment, he will be able to fix his monthly payment at £200 for the period of the loan. In order to do this, he must know what rate of interest will fix his payment at exactly £200.

After using the spreadsheet program's goalseeking function, he determines that the rate of interest must be 6.02% before the monthly repayment becomes precisely £200. In activating the goalseeking function, he carried out the following steps:

* the Input cell was set to B5 which contained the current interest rate. This is the value that would need to be altered in order to achieve the result he required.

* the Output cell was set to B7 which contained the original @PMT function and which was used to display the first answer he obtained (£223.17).

* the Desired Value was entered as 200 since this was the maximum monthly payment he was prepared to make

* the Tolerance was set at 0.01, to ensure that the answer was accurate to within 1% (or 1 penny)

	A	B
1	GOALSEEKING EXAMPLE	
2	___________	
3		
4	LOAN:	£18,000.00
5	INTEREST RATE:	6.02%
6	TERM (MONTHS):	120
7	PAYMENT:	£200.00

Although the answer could have been reached using several other methods, none are as efficient as the program's goalseeking function. Where more complex problems are dealt with, savings in time and labour are substantial. The ability to specify different tolerance levels can be used to increase the speed of the calculation or ensure the maximum possible accuracy.

8.7 Creating data input forms

When creating simple database applications within a spreadsheet program, ease of use can be improved by creating custom input forms for users to complete. Such forms can be created in seconds by using the program's built-in function. Alternatively, a macro could be used to create and activate a data input form automatically.

* Enter a number of headings that will be used to title the different fields in your data table

* Format each column to display the data it will contain in the correct format

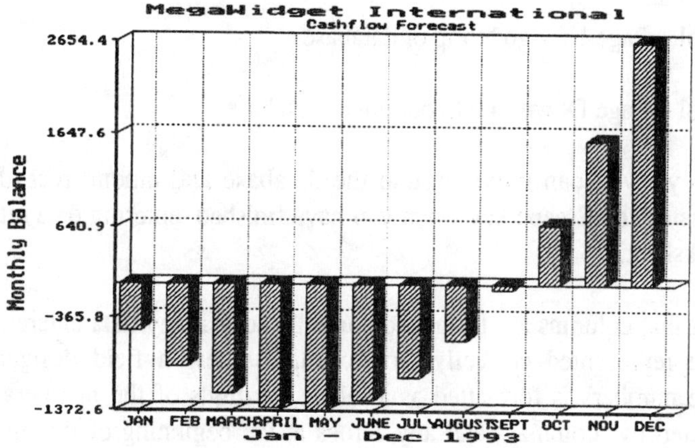

* Select "Data" from the main menu to enter the Data sub-menu

* Select "Input" to enter the Database Input sub-menu

* Select "Form" and then highlight the row of column headings you created

The abbreviated form of this command is "/DIF".

The data input form is then created and the worksheet is prepared to accept data for your database. The cell pointer is positioned at first entry in the data table and after each record is entered, the cell pointer will be automatically repositioned to the beginning of the next blank entry. The following keys can also be used when working in this mode:

* Escape - quit the data input routine

* Page Up - previous record

* Page Down - next record

* Cursor Up (*) - previous field

* Cursor Down (*) - next field

* Cursor Left/Right - edit field

* Control + Page Up - go to top of database

* Control + Page Down - go to bottom of database

Using these keys, you can move around the database and amend records as necessary. Pressing the Escape key when you have finished entering data returns you to the worksheet.

It is important that columns are formatted correctly so that any data entered into a field will be represented correctly. For example, unless a field designed to hold telephone numbers is formatted as a label, the digits of the numbers will become separated by commas and any zeroes at the beginning of the number will be lost.

Some programs place restrictions on the use of data input forms, including the maximum width of field names, the maximum number of fields allowed in a data input form and the way in which fields are formatted. However, this technique is generally flexible enough to cater for most basic applications.

8.8 Finding and extracting records

There are two methods of retrieving information from a completed database. *Finding* records involves highlighting any records that match a given set of conditions. *Extracting* records involves copying a set of records that match a given set of conditions to another location. These commands operate by using three ranges of cells:

* Input range - this defines the section of the database to be searched. Each section highlighted should include the field name (the title of the column).

* Output range - this defines the area where results are to be stored for an extract operation. The correct number of columns should be reserved for the data and column headings should match those of the Input range.

* Criterion range - this defines the area containing the conditions of the find or extract operation. Again, the column headings should match those used in the database.

Essentially, three areas of the worksheet are reserved for find and extract operations; the database itself, an area to store the results of extract operations and an area to hold the search conditions. The search operation works by comparing the contents of individual records with a set of search strings supplied by the user. Where matches are found, records are either highlighted or copied to a new location.

The search conditions can be specified using the following special characters:

* ? - substitutes for any one character in the comparison string

* * - substitutes for all of the characters to the right of the asterisk

* ... - (three full stops) if this precedes a string, the search will locate the string anywhere in a record

* ~ - (tilde) searches for records that does not contain the string that follows

* logical operators - (e.g. <, >= etc.) can be used for numeric comparisons.

```
NAME          ADDRESS
TELEPHONE
J*            ...Baker
6*
M*            ...Baker
6*
```

Additionally, AND and OR comparisons can be carried out by placing additional conditions in adjacent rows and columns. For example, the search conditions above could be interpreted as:

> Select all records where the entry in Name begins with a "J" AND where Address contains the string "Baker" AND where the Telephone number begins with a "6". Additionally (OR), look for those records where Name begins with "M" AND Address contains the string "Baker" AND where Telephone number begins with a "6".

The commands are activated as follows:

* Select "Data" from the main menu

* Select "Question" from the Data sub-menu

* Select "Input" and highlight the database to be searched (including column headings)

* If about to use the Extract command, select "Output" and highlight the area to be used for extracted records. Only the column headings need to be highlighted.

* Select "Criterion" and highlight the Criterion Range (including column headings)

* Select "Find" or "Extract"

The abbreviated form of this command is "/DQE" or "/DQF".

The following example demonstrates how both find and extract operations are performed. The crude database below represents a simple address book application.

```
EXTRACT-SORT EXAMPLE
____________

NAME          ADDRESS                  TELEPHONE

J. Smith      1 Acacia Avenue          345612
G. Rafferty   27 Baker Street          456123
I. Brennan    17 Coronation Street     612345
M. Mortimer   Crossroads Motel         234561
S. Holmes     221-223 Baker Street     654321
C. Smith      17 Surbiton Road         654123
```

Assuming that we want to find all of those people named "Smith", we would establish a Criterion Range where the "Name" field contained "Smith". The other fields could be left empty since we have no further conditions for the search.

The worksheet now looks like this:

```
EXTRACT-SORT EXAMPLE
____________

NAME          ADDRESS                  TELEPHONE
J. Smith      1 Acacia Avenue          345612
G. Rafferty   27 Baker Street          456123
I. Brennan    17 Coronation Street     612345
M. Mortimer   Crossroads Motel         234561
S. Holmes     221-223 Baker Street     654321
C. Smith      17 Surbiton Road         654123

NAME          ADDRESS                  TELEPHONE
...Smith      *                        *
```

The Criterion Range (at the bottom of the illustration) instructs the program to look for records where the "Name" field contains "Smith" in any position. The asterisks in the "Address" and "Telephone" fields mean that any data in these areas is acceptable. The result of this search highlights "J. Smith" and "C. Smith".

A slightly more complex search might be easier to perform if the results can be stored in a separate area of the worksheet. This time, we wish to locate anyone with the surname of "Mortimer" and anyone who lives on Baker Street. Using the Extract command, the worksheet appears as shown below:

```
EXTRACT-SORT EXAMPLE
--------------------
NAME          ADDRESS                  TELEPHONE
J. Smith      1 Acacia Avenue          345612
G. Rafferty   27 Baker Street          456123
I. Brennan    17 Coronation Street     612345
M. Mortimer   Crossroads Motel         234561
S. Holmes     221-223 Baker Street     654321
C. Smith      17 Surbiton Road         654123

SEARCH CRITERIA
---------------
NAME          ADDRESS                  TELEPHONE
...Mortimer   *                        *
*             ...Baker                 *

EXTRACTED RECORDS
-----------------
NAME          ADDRESS                  TELEPHONE
M. Mortimer   Crossroads Motel         234561
G. Rafferty   27 Baker Street          456123
S. Holmes     221-223 Baker Street     654321
```

8.9 Three-dimensional worksheets

A standard worksheet is considered to be two-dimensional in that it has only vertical and horizontal co- ordinates. However, it is possible to simulate a three-dimensional environment by splitting a worksheet into a number of separate pages. This can be extremely useful in a number of situations, for example when making historical comparisons or creating a complex application from self-contained modules.

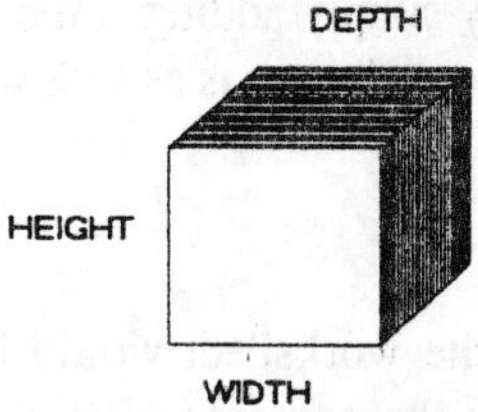

To create a number of panels, the following procedure is used:

* From the main menu, select Worksheet

* From the Worksheet sub-menu, select "General"

* From the General sub-menu, select "Install"

* Select "Dimension" and enter the number of pages you wish to use

The abbreviated form of this command is "/WGID".

The worksheet is now divided into a number of equal pages, each numbered alphabetically. These pages can be reached by simply moving around the worksheet in the normal way. Additionally, two other keystroke commands are provided for more rapid movement:

* Control + Page Up - Move to the previous page

* Control + Page Down - Move to the next page

You can remove extra pages by repeating the steps given above and restoring the worksheet to a single page. Since the position of any additional pages is relative to the main worksheet area, no data will be lost; it will merely remain in the same area of the worksheet.

A cell in a new page can be accessed by simply adding some additional data to its co-ordinate. The format for page co-ordinates is as follows:

PAGE:CO-ORDINATE

For example, cell B25 on page K of the worksheet would be identified with "K:B25". Thus, "+K:B25" would copy the contents of B25 on page K to the current cell. Additionally, commands such as @SUM(A:A100..E:A100) are also valid, allowing "3D" calculations to be made.

This technique allows worksheets to be used both in isolation and together. The most common use for "3D" worksheets is for making historical comparisons. For example, the same basic worksheet could be copied to a number of pages and used to analyse an employee's expenses from, say, 1988 to 1993. Each page would contain a separate annual expense report and each report could be analysed separately before being studied together as a whole.

8.10 Summary

In this section, you have learned how to:

* construct data tables
* automatically fill cells with values ascending or descending by regular amounts
* automatically generate tables of values
* sort data
* produce frequency distribution tables
* use goalseeking functions
* create data input forms
* find and extract data from database applications
* use three-dimensional worksheets

Section 9: Working With Spreadsheets

9.1 Objective

It is impossible to work with spreadsheets in a way that does not involve at least some use of the computer's operating system. Even graphical user interfaces (GUI), such as Windows 3.1, require the user to have some basic knowledge of MS-DOS. The purpose of this section is to introduce users to some basic procedures that will improve productivity and increase data security. The last part of this section describes a number of MS-DOS commands that are likely to be of use to most people. These commands can be used to manage worksheet files so that adequate security copies can be made. For more information on MS-DOS, refer to the user guide that accompanies every copy of the software. Alternatively, users of MS-DOS version 5 can type "HELP" on the command line for a brief description of the available commands.

9.2 The importance of backing up data

Any spreadsheet project involves an investment of time and labour. In commercial environments, the development of a worksheet usually equates to a significant investment in terms of money. With this in mind, it is important that precautions are taken against the possibility of data loss.

There are three major ways in which data loss can occur. These can be summarised as follows:

* Accidental damage. This includes areas such as accidental erasure, power loss, defective media, breakdowns and spillages.

* Deliberate acts of damage. This includes vandalism and sabotage.

* Virus attacks. Certain computer viruses target data files in a variety of ways, ranging from encrypting text files to erasing the entire contents of a floppy or hard disk.

Essentially, the value of back up procedures is that they minimise the risk of a total loss of data and allow recovery to take place with a minimum of time, effort and expense.

9.3 Grandfather, father, son

One of the most common methods of protecting valuable data is to use the "grandfather, father, son" technique. Here, a rotating set of back up disks is used so that three different versions of the same data are held at any one time.

To illustrate this method, imagine a single user working with a personal computer and using three floppy disks to store his or her data on. Each day, all of the data being worked on is copied onto the disk containing the oldest version ("grandfather") of that data. This creates a continuous cycle that ensures that the oldest back up is never more than 3 days old. The table below shows how the method works:

DAY 1	DAY 2	DAY 3	DAY 4	DAY 5
Disk 1 Grandfather	Disk 2 Grandfather	Disk 3 Grandfather	Disk 1 Grandfather	Disk 2 Grandfather
Disk 2 Father	Disk 3 Father	Disk 1 Father	Disk 2 Father	Disk 3 Father
Disk 3 Son	Disk 1 Son	Disk 2 Son	Disk 3 Son	Disk 1 Son

As you can see, each disk moves through three "generations". The major advantages of this method can be summarised as follows:

* Three back up disks mean that it is almost impossible to lose all of your data. The risk of all 3 back up copies failing is so small as to be negligible.

* Normally, only a single day's work would be lost if the original data became corrupted or was destroyed. Even if the "son" and "father" back up copies failed, only two day's work would be lost.

9.4 Some guidelines for back up procedures

The following is a brief list of important guidelines to consider when implementing back up procedures:

* Back ups are almost useless unless made regularly. How often back ups are

made depends largely upon the amount of work processed. As a general rule, back ups should be made at least once a day.

* The back up copies should be kept at a different location from the master copy.

* The integrity of all back up copies should be checked when they are made and access to these copies should be restricted. This is to prevent accidental or even deliberate harm coming to the copies.

There are two basic ways of backing up data. The first is to manually copy all of the files onto a floppy disk, magnetic tape or a removable data cartridge. This can be done via the File Manager in Windows or by using the COPY and XCOPY commands in MS-DOS (see Copying Files). The second method involves the use of commercial back up software which offers a number of advantages over manual copying. For example, back up programs can be set to perform full or partial back ups automatically at pre-set intervals. For most users, a floppy disk is normally more than adequate for storing even the largest spreadsheet file.

9.5 What is a computer virus?

A computer virus is a small program that is designed to infiltrate a computer system and spread copies of itself wherever possible.

Viruses infect floppy disks, hard disks, network servers and memory. Contrary to popular belief all viruses can be harmful to a computer system, even if they do nothing more than display a comical message. The more malignant varieties of virus programs deliberately seek to destroy valuable program and data files. It is for this reason that effective security measures are essential.

9.6 Precautions against viruses

There are a number of precautions that can be taken against virus attacks. The majority of these precautions cost nothing to implement and can be carried out by any user.

The first method is to restrict unauthorised or unnecessary access to sensitive data and equipment. The fewer people that are capable of accessing the data, the less likely it is that one of them might introduce a virus into the system (accidentally or deliberately). Unauthorised software, such as games, and pirate software is a major source of virus infection. Preventing this kind of software from being installed on the system can go a long way to reducing the risk of infection.

Keep all floppy disks write-protected whenever possible. The older 5.25" disk can be write-protected by sticking an adhesive label over a notch on the edge of the disk. A 3.5" disk is write-protected when the plastic write-protect tab is open (i.e. you can see daylight through the hole). Once a disk has been write- protected a virus is unable to copy itself to that disk.

Never introduce unknown software into the system. For example, if a floppy disk arrives through the post from an unknown sender, only a fool would use the disk on his or her system without first checking it thoroughly.

Use a virus detection program regularly to scan the system for possible infections. Such programs are available at extremely low cost and are an excellent investment. If possible, install an antivirus program (sometimes known as a virus shield). These programs constantly monitor the system and alert the user if a virus attempts to copy itself to a disk.

If practical, cold boot the computer in between using different applications. This involves physically switching the power off to the machine for a reasonable period of time, say, 15 - 30 seconds. The reason for this is because some viruses remain in memory until the machine is shut down and many can survive a brief power loss to the computer.

9.7 Dealing with viruses

Sometimes, the only way a virus infection is detected is when the system begins to behave strangely. For example, if the machine slows down or uses the hard disk at a time when it normally wouldn't, these might indicate infection.

If the computer starts to behave differently, investigate the possibility of a virus infection immediately.

As already mentioned, a virus detection program is probably the most effective way of locating and dealing with viruses. Most programs contain a utility called a virus killer. These programs offer several ways of removing viruses ranging from repairing infected files to deleting them so that there is no possibility of recovery.

If a virus is detected, do not use the machine until the virus has been removed.

Once the virus has been removed, check the entire system in case the virus has been able to copy itself to another location. For example, you might erase a virus from memory but it may well have already written a copy of itself to the hard drive. In this case, the next time the machine is switched on, the virus will load from the hard disk and the machine will become infected once more. If the machine is part of a network, you must also check all of the other machines attached to the network and the file server.

If you are unsure of how to remove a computer virus, seek expert help immediately.

9.8 The directory structure of a disk

The structure of any disk is arranged in a number of levels. The topmost level is normally called the root directory. All lower levels are known as sub directories. Users of machines such as the Atari STE will often hear sub-directories referred to as "folders". Since it is felt that this is a more suitable term, it is used throughout this section.

Sub directories may themselves contain one or more other directories. In this case, the main directory is known as the parent and the others are known as children.

The directory structure can contain many branches and sub-branches. The way in which a directory is arranged is often known as a directory tree.

The root directory is signified by a system prompt which might appear as A: or B: If a sub directory is currently selected, the system prompt will change appearance. For example, it might be A:\WINWORD\ or C:\DOS\

The system of sub directories might be compared to a filing cabinet. The cabinet itself is the root directory since all other drawers, folders and documents are stored within it. The drawers and folders are sub directories - the drawers are parents and the folders are children. Finally, the documents within each folder are individual files.

9.9 The CD command

The Change Directory command in MS DOS allows you to move around the directory structure of the disk you are working with. The command can be used in three main ways:

```
CD (Directory Name)
CD..
CD\
```

The first command allows you to move into a specified sub directory. For example, CD ASEASYAS would move you inside the sub directory called ASEASYAS. If ASEASYAS contained a further sub directory, say, SHEETS, you could move directly to it from the root directory with:

```
CD\ASEASYAS\SHEETS
```

Additionally, you may specify full path names so that you can move from one disk to another. For example, if you were currently on the A drive, CD C:\ASEASYAS\SHEETS would move you onto the C drive and into the SHEETS folder.

It is important to note that if you are moving from one sub directory to another, the "\" character must follow directly after the CD command.

Note also that commands operate locally when inside a folder. For example, if the logged sub directory was SHEETS, the command COPY A:*.* C: would copy everything from the A disk into the SHEETS folder (and not onto the root directory as you might expect). Similarly, DEL *.* would delete only the files within the current directory and would leave all other files and sub directories unaffected.

The command CD.. moves back up one level in the directory structure. Again, if we were in SHEETS, the command would move us back up to ASEASYAS.

The command CD\ returns to the root directory of the current drive.

9.10 Working with directories

When you load a normal DOS program from a hard disk or floppy disk, the current directory will normally be changed to the program's location. For example, if you were using AsEasyAs, the current directory might be C:\ASEASYAS

It is always a good idea to create a separate sub directory to store your data files in. This can be easily achieved by using the command:

```
MKDIR (Directory Name)
```

The MKDIR command creates a new sub directory in the current location. For example, if you were already in C:\ASEASYAS and issued the command MKDIR SHEETS, a new sub directory would be created inside the ASEASYAS directory.

A directory can be removed by using the command:

```
RMDIR (Directory Name)
```

Remember that the directory to be removed must be empty otherwise the command will return an error message.

Incidentally, to view a graphic representation of the directory tree of the current drive, use the command TREE /A.

9.11 The DIR command

This command has the format:

DIR File Specification /Switches

Using DIR on its own will display all files in the current directory.

9.12 The file specification

The file specification allows the user to determine precisely which files should be listed. A file name can be up to eight characters in length and can have an extension of up to three characters in length. Thus, the following file names are all valid:

```
LETTER.DOC
L.DOC
L.D
LETTER
```

Two characters ("wild cards") may be used to format the file specification so that groups of similar files may be viewed. The asterisk (*) represents a group of letters and the interrogation mark (?) represents any single character. The asterisk represents all characters between itself and the end of the file name or extension.

For example, LETTE*.DOC means "all files with the first characters LETTE, followed by up to 3 other characters (any), followed by an extension of DOC". In other words, such a specification used in a directory listing would list files such as LETTEAAA.DOC, LETTEBBB.DOC , LETTE123.DOC and so forth.

If the specification *.DOC was to be used, all files ending with the extension of DOC would be listed. Similarly, if the specification LETTER.* was used, all files called LETTER would be listed, regardless of the extension.

The asterisk can be taken as meaning: "any characters from this position to the end of the file name (or extension)".

Asterisks can be used to mean "all files" with: *.* In this way, DEL *.* would delete every file in the current directory.

The interrogation mark can be used to represent any one character in any part of the file name. Thus, ?ETTER.DOC would locate all files containing "ETTER.DOC", regardless of the first letter in the file name.

The interrogation mark means "any one character".

Applying this to the DIR command, we can now, say, list only those files ending with the extension 'DOC':

```
DIR *.DOC
```

...Or any file beginning with the letter A and ending with the extension "DOC":

```
DIR A*.DOC
```

...Or any file containing the letters "WK" in the extension:

```
DIR *.WK?
```

Note that a question mark should not be used following an asterisk in the same part of the file name. For example, the command DIR *???.* would be illegal, as would DIR *.*??

A file specification can also include a path. For example, DIR A:\DOC\LETTER.* would display all files with the name of LETTER, regardless of extension, in the DOC directory on drive A.

9.13 DIR command switches

There are two basic switches that can be used with the DIR command. A switch is a minor modification to a command which causes it to behave in a slightly different way. A switch is normally applied by using "/" followed by a command letter:

```
DIR /P
DIR /W
```

The first command instructs the computer to display a full screen of directory entries and to then wait until a key is pressed before showing the next screen. The "P" stands for "Pause". Thus, DIR *.* /P would show every file in the current directory, pausing at the end of each page to allow the user to examine the listing properly.

The second command instructs the computer to display the directory across the screen, as opposed from top to bottom. This abbreviates the information which is displayed about each file but allows far more entries to be shown on a single screen. The "W" stands for "Wide".

9.14 Storing files

Although File Manager in Windows is a more convenient method of copying files, directories and disks, it has to be recognised that Windows itself is not available on all machines (in fact, estimates suggest that fewer than 10% of machines use Windows at all). For this reason, it is important that all users get to grips with the MS-DOS copying commands: COPY, XCOPY and DISKCOPY.

As mentioned earlier, it is preferable to keep data files stored in a separate location from the program that created them. Normally, this is done by storing the program itself on the hard disk and the data files on floppy disks. Many people simply create a separate sub directory on their hard disk for data and back the entire directory up at the end of each working day. For example, a fairly common convention is to use a sub directory called "SHEETS" on the hard disk for storing spreadsheet files. At the end of the day, the entire contents of the sub directory can be copied onto a floppy disk with a single MS-DOS command.

9.15 Formatting a data disk

Before you can make back up copies or use a data disk, it must be formatted using the MS-DOS FORMAT command. This command prepares a disk to receive data by creating a "map" of its structure for the computer to use.

The FORMAT command is quite complex and has a number of variations. For the purpose of creating a data disk or back up disk, the following format description is sufficient:

```
FORMAT [DRIVE] [QUICK] [SIZE]
```

The drive is simply the identification letter of the drive containing the disk to be formatted.

The "Quick" switch is used to specify a quick format or an unconditional format. If the disk has been used before, it is not necessary to carry out a full format again. Normally, MS-DOS will recognise the fact that a disk has previously been formatted and will automatically carry out a quick format. If it does not, a "/Q" switch can be added to the command line to speed up the formatting process. On the other hand, if you want the disk to have a full format, "/U" tells the computer to ignore any existing format data on the disk and carry out the full formatting procedure.

Disk Type	Capacity	Command Switch
5.25" Standard	360K	/F:360
5.25" High Density	1.2Mb	/F:1.2
3.5" Standard	720K	/F:720
3.5" High Density	1.44Mb	/F:1.44

The size of the disk is determined by using the "/F:" switch together with a number representing the storage capacity of the disk. The table gives the relevant capacities of standard floppy disks and the format of the switch to use with the FORMAT command.

As an example, here is the command to carry out an unconditional format of a standard 3.5" disk located in the A: drive:

```
FORMAT A: /U /F:720
```

The following carries out a quick format on a high density 5.25" disk in drive B:

```
FORMAT B: /Q /F:1.2
```

At the end of each formatting process, you will be asked if you wish to specify a volume name for the disk. This is merely a name that will allow you to identify the disk when viewing its directory. For example, a DIR command might produce the message "Volume in drive A is MYLETTERS..." followed by the contents of the disk. A volume name is optional but, if a name is entered, it must be not be longer than 11 characters.

You must not use the FORMAT command on a hard drive - this might result in physical damage to some units and will erase all of the data stored on the drive.

9.16 The COPY command

COPY can be used to copy individual files or entire groups of files to a new location. The basic format of the command is as follows:

```
COPY [SOURCE] [DESTINATION]
```

The source specifies the file(s) you want to copy. The destination specifies where you want to place the new copy or copies. Perhaps a better way of showing the command's format is this:

```
COPY [FROM where...] [TO where...]
```

If a path name is not given in the source description, the command assumes that the current path should be used. For example, if you are currently in C:\WINDOWS and issue the command without a path name, the computer assumes that the files you want to copy will be found in the WINDOWS sub directory. Since files can not be copied onto themselves, you must specify a new location or a new name for the destination copy. In other words, you will normally copy files to another sub directory or disk drive. However, if you want to make an identical copy of a file and store it in the same location as the original, you must give the new copy a unique name of its own. Thus, COPY A:\AUTOEXEC.BAT A: is illegal since it requests the computer to copy a file onto itself. On the other hand, COPY A:\AUTOEXEC.BAT A:\AUTO.BAT is fine since the new copy of AUTOEXEC.BAT will have a new, unique name (AUTO.BAT).

If your system has only one floppy drive, the computer can still make disk-to-disk copies. All that happens is that the computer reads a file or files from the source disk and then asks you to replace it with the destination disk. The process is punctuated by a series of simple instructions and is relatively simple to follow. For example, the first instruction is usually "Insert SOURCE disk in drive A: Press a key to continue." When an amount of data has been copied, a new instruction appears: "Insert DESTINATION disk in drive A: Press a key to continue." This continues until the copying process has been completed.

Assuming that we are in the root directory of the hard disk (C:\), here are some examples of the COPY command in use:

```
COPY AUTOEXEC.BAT A:
```

The computer assumes that the source directory is the current one and copies the Autoexec.Bat file to the root directory of the A: disk drive.

```
COPY C:\WINDOWS\CHIMES.WAV A:\SOUNDS
```

This time, the computer searches in the WINDOWS sub directory for a file called Chimes.Wav and then copies it into the SOUNDS sub directory on the A: disk drive.

```
COPY C:\WINDOWS\CHIMES.WAV A:\SOUNDS\BARS.WAV
```

This final examples works in exactly the same way as the previous one except for one important difference. This time, we have specified a new file name for the copy; it will be renamed from Chimes.Wav to Bars.Wav.

9.17 Copying groups of files

Wild cards can be used with the COPY command to specify that whole groups of files should be copied in one operation (see the DIR command for more information).

Essentially, the interrogation mark (?) can be used to represent any single character in the file name whilst the asterisk (*) can be used to represent any group of characters from the position of the asterisk to the end of the file name or extension.

Again, here are a few examples of how this can be used:

```
COPY *.WKS A:
```

Spreadsheet files created with programs compatible with Lotus 1-2-3 tend to end with an extension of ".WKS" or ".WK1". Rather than copy each file individually, all of the files ending with ".WKS" can be copied by using an asterisk to represent the first part of the file name. In this example, all worksheet files are copied from the current location to the root directory of the A: disk drive.

```
COPY LETTER?.DOC A:
```

In this example, imagine that we have a number of letters called LETTER1, LETTER2... and so on. The interrogation mark takes the place of any character in that particular position of the file name. Since an exact match must be made with the remainder of the file name before the file will be copied, this command would have the effect of copying all of these letters to the root directory of the A: drive in a single operation.

```
COPY *.* A:
```

Since the asterisk can be used to represent any group of characters, this example copies every file in the current location to the A: drive.

9.18 Verifying copies

There are a number of command switches that can added to the COPY command to modify its actions. The only one of any real importance is the "V" switch, which ensures that each copy made matches the original file exactly. Although disk and file errors are relatively uncommon during copying operations, it is wise to make absolutely certain that only accurate copies have been made. This is especially important if making back ups of important data.

The "Verify" switch is used by simply adding it to the end of the COPY command line, separating it with a "/" character:

COPY [Source] [Destination] /V

9.19 The XCOPY command

The XCOPY command reduces the number of disk swaps needed to copy a number of files. It has the additional benefit of being able to reproduce the directory tree (directory structure) of the source disk onto the destination disk.

The command takes the following format:

```
XCOPY [SOURCE] [DESTINATION]
```

As with COPY, path names and wild cards can be used to include or exclude entire groups of files. However, it should be remembered that XCOPY is not suitable for renaming destination files.

Here is an example of how XCOPY works:

```
XCOPY C:\WINDOWS\*.* A:\
```

In this case, the command copies all of the files in the Windows directory of the C: drive onto the A: drive. Unlike COPY, a quantity of files are read at a time so the process is quicker and requires far fewer disk swaps.

A number of switches can be used to modify the way in which XCOPY works. Only three of these are of any real importance: "V", "E" and "S". The "V" switch verifies that all of the copies made are exact reproductions of the source files. "E" copies the directory tree (structure) of the source directory, including empty sub directories. The "S" switch copies the directory tree of the source directory but ignores empty sub directories. An example might help to make this a little clearer.

Imagine that a sub directory, C:\DOCUMENT, contains three other sub directories; TEXT, LETTERS and INVOICES. Of these three, TEXT is empty. The others (including DOCUMENT) contain a variety of files, ranging from business letters to large reports. Here's how the "E" and "S" switches would work:

```
XCOPY C:\DOCUMENT\*.* A: /E
```

This would create a DOCUMENT sub directory on the A: drive and also create the TEXT, LETTERS and INVOICES sub directories. In other words, the TEXT sub directory would be reproduced even though it is empty. All of the files in all of the sub directories of DOCUMENT on C: would be copied into their respective positions on A:.

```
XCOPY C:\DOCUMENT\*.* A: /S
```

The "S" switch would work in exactly the same way except that the TEXT sub directory would not be created since it is empty and therefore unnecessary.

Note that COPY and XCOPY work with formatted disks only. Additionally, if there is insufficient disk space available for the copies to be stored, the process will fail.

9.20 The DISKCOPY command

An entire disk can be copied by using the DISKCOPY command. Once again, the command takes the format:

```
DISKCOPY [SOURCE] [DESTINATION]
```

Just as with COPY and XCOPY, the same drive can be used to "pretend" it is both the source and destination disk drive. The most common way of using DISKCOPY is:

```
DISKCOPY A: B: /V
```

This creates an exact copy of the disk in drive A: on drive B: There are, however, two important points to note here. Firstly, both disks must be of exactly the same type (size and capacity). In other words, it is not possible to copy the contents of a 5.25" disk onto a 3.5" disk using this command (if you wanted to do this, you would format both disks and then copy all of the files using XCOPY). Secondly, the "V" switch should always be used to verify the accuracy of each copy since a corrupted disk is far more serious that a single corrupted file.

9.21 Deleting files

You may need to delete files in order to replace them with more recent versions. This can be done by using the DELETE command.

```
DEL [PATH NAME/FILE NAME]
```

The DELETE command uses a simple file specification in order to identify the files to be erased. Wild cards are allowed, as is a complete file path. Here are two examples:

```
DEL *.*
```

This deletes all of the files in the current directory.

```
DEL A:\LETTER\*.DOC
```

This deletes all of the files with the extension of ".DOC" in the LETTER sub directory on drive A.

If you accidentally delete a file it can often be recovered by using the UNDELETE command. The basic format of the command is:

```
UNDELETE [FILE PATH/NAME]
```

You must give the full path and file name of the file to be recovered. Note that if you have stored any new files on your disk or made any other changes to the contents of the disk, an UNDELETE operation is not likely to succeed.

9.22 Copying with Windows

File Manager in Windows 3.0 and 3.1 simplifies the process of copying files and disks.

There is little need to described copying with Windows in detail due to the availability of File Manager's excellent built-in help system. However, two simple hints might be useful to most users:

* Copying can be made easier by opening two windows in File Manager, using one to highlight the source and the other to specify the destination.

* For machines with only one floppy drive, copying can be made quicker by creating a temporary directory on the hard disk. In this way, files can be copied onto the hard drive, the destination disk can be placed into the disk drive and the files can be copied back out again. This removes the need for constant disk swapping.

9.23 Command summary

*can be used with wild cards

CD [DIRECTORY] Changes to another directory.

Variations: CD.. Move one level upwards in the directory structure

CD Return to the root directory of the current drive

CD\Directory Change to a new sub directory regardless of current position

***COPY [SOURCE] [DESTINATION] /V** Copies a file or files from location to another.

Switches: /V Verifies the accuracy of the copy made.

***DEL [FILE PATH/NAME]** Deletes a file or group of files.

***DIR [FILE PATH/NAME] /P /W** Show directory listing (behaves exactly the same as DIR *.*)

Switches: /P Pause after each page of information /W Display wide format listing

***XCOPY [SOURCE] [DESTINATION] /V /S /E** Copies a file or group of files to another location. Faster than COPY and allows the tree structure to be reproduced in the target location.

Switches: /V Verifies the accuracy of the copy made /S Copies the tree structure, ignoring empty sub directories /E Copies the tree structure including empty sub directories

FORMAT [DRIVE] [QUICK] [SIZE] Prepares a disk for use with a computer.

Switches: **/Q** Attempts a quick format of the disk
/U Unconditional format of the disk
/F:SIZE Specifies the capacity of the disk

MKDIR [DIRECTORY] Create a new sub directory

RMDIR [DIRECTORY] Delete an empty sub directory

TREE /A View a diagram of the directory structure

***UNDELETE [FILE PATH/NAME]** Attempts to recover a file or group of files after a DEL command has been carried out.

"WILD CARDS" ? Represents any single character in the file name or extension * Represents any group of characters from the position of the asterisk to the end of the file name or extension

9.24 Summary

In this section you have learned how to:

* follow an established back up procedure for important data files
* protect important data files from accidental and deliberate damage
* prevent infection by computer viruses
* use MS-DOS commands including DIR, CD, COPY, DISKCOPY, XCOPY, FORMAT and MKDIR

Reference List

Appendix 1

AsEasyAs and AsEasyAs Lite

Trius Incorporated produces two major spreadsheet products that are to be highly recommended for all general purposes. AsEasyAs is the equal of almost any other package and is quite capable of handling even the most demanding tasks. AsEasyAs Lite is a cut-down version of the program and is an ideal first step for beginners before moving onto more sophisticated packages. Both programs are made even more attractive by their extremely low prices.

These programs have been specially recommended for the following reasons:

* Low cost. Both programs cost a fraction of the price of their rivals.

* Lotus 1-2-3 compatibility. Both programs are highly compatible with Lotus 1-2-3, with only relatively minor differences in their features and menu structures.

* Ease of use. The Shareware versions of both programs come complete with detailed manuals (as text files on disk) and feature full on-line, context-sensitive help. Registered versions of each program have printed manuals.

* Performance. Both programs perform significantly better than many of their rivals and are the equal of most others.

* Hardware requirements. Early versions of both programs will work on a minimal PC system, requiring only a single-sided disk drive and 256K of memory. However, please note that versions 5.0 and 5.1 are the latest incarnations of AsEasyAs and require 384K of free memory and at least one double-sided disk drive.

* Both products are distributed as Shareware, meaning that they can be evaluated over a trial period of 30 days before they must be registered.

The Shareware versions of each program are available from most Public Domain libraries and bulletin board systems. Evaluation copies are free of charge, although there will be a small copying and postage fee if the software is ordered from a Public Domain library.

Current registration fees are approximately £45 for AsEasyAs and £19 for AsEasyAs Lite. American registration fees will vary but will be along the lines of $50 for AsEasyAs and $25 for AsEasyAs Lite.

In the UK, copies of each program can be obtained from Shareware Publishing and The Public Domain Software Library. Shareware Publishing are the official distributors for Trius products in the United Kingdom. The company offers a foreign registration service that allows customers to buy registered versions of the programs without having to send their fees abroad.

Shareware Publishing,
3a Queen Street,
Seaton,
Devon,
EX12 2NY.

Tel: (0297) 24088

The Public Domain Software Library,
Winscombe House,
Beacon Road,
Crowborough,
Sussex,
TN6 1UL.

Tel: (0892) 663298

Please note that if you intend to use the software on a regular basis, you are legally obliged to register your copy. In order to encourage registrations, Trius offers the following benefits to users:

* A registered copy of the latest version of the program.

* A printed and bound user manual.

* Technical support.

* A subscription to the company's newsletter.

In addition to these benefits, you are likely to be offered future software upgrades at discounted prices and receive special offers on any of the company's other products.

TRIUS Inc.
231 Sutton Street, Suite 2D-3
P.O. Box 249
North Andover,
MA 01845-1639
U.S.A. Tel. (508) 794-9377

Appendix 2

Macro Key Words

Basic Commands

The following is a list of common macro key words. The specific format of any command may vary from package to package. Refer to your program user manual for more information.

{LT} - Moves the cursor to the left*

{RT} - Moves the cursor to the right*

{DN} - Moves the cursor downwards*

{UP} - Moves the cursor upwards*

{PGUP} - Moves the cursor one page up at a time*

{PGDN} - Moves the cursor one page down at a time*

{PGRT} - Moves the cursor one page right at a time*

{PGLT} - Moves the cursor one page left at a time*

{DEL} - Deletes a character (from the right of the cursor)*

{BS} - Backspace (delete) a character (from the left of the cursor)*

{INS} - Toggles between Insert and Overwrite modes (simulates the INS key)

{INSON} - Turns Insert mode on

{INSOFF} - Turns Insert mode off (Overwrite)

{HOME} - Simulates the HOME key

{END} - Simulates the END key

{EDIT} - Brings the contents of the current cell onto the edit line (simulates F2)

{NAME} - Show names (simulates F3)

{ABS} - Makes the current cell reference absolute (simulates F4)

{GOTO Co-ordinate} - Moves to a specified location (simulates F5)

{WINDOW} - If two windows are open, this toggles between them. Otherwise, it toggles the position of the cursor between its current and last positions (simulates F6)

{VIEW} - Toggles between views of the current windows (simulates F7)

{CALC} - Recalculate the worksheet (simulates F9)

{GRAPH} - Displays the current graph (simulates F10)

{ESC X} - Simulates the Escape key*

~ - Simulates the Enter key

An asterisk (*) denotes that the command can be repeated by including a value with key word, usually in the form: {KEYWORD VALUE}.

Advanced Commands

The commands listed here are relevant to AsEasyAs Version 5.00. Older packages are unlikely to support many of the facilities described here and the format of any similar commands will almost certainly be different. Refer to your program user manual for more information.

{?}
Pauses macro execution until the Enter or ESC key is pressed. This command can be used to allow movement around the worksheet or data entry.

{APPEND F#, "FileName"}
F# - File Number (from 1 to 5)
"FileName" - Name of file, with or without drive and path information

Opens a file in Append mode (see {OPEN}), allowing text to be appended to the end of the file with the {WRITE} command. Note: files opened with this command MUST be closed before exiting the program or the file will become corrupted.

{BEEP X}
Produces a beep sound.

{BLANK Range}
Erases the cells defined by "Range". This is the equivalent of "/RE".

{BORDEROFF}
Switches column and row borders off. This is the equivalent of "/SBS". The effect lasts until a {BORDERON} command is used.

{BORDERON}
Cancels the effect of {BORDEROFF}. The screen should be updated by using the {UPDATE} command after {BORDERON} has been used.

{CALL Location or RangeName}
Executes the subroutine at "Location" or "RangeName". When a {RET} command is encountered, control returns to the command directly after the {CALL} command. Nested subroutines, up to 20 levels deep, may be used.

{CLOSE F#}
F# - File Number (from 1 to 5)

Closes disk file F#.

{CLRSCR}

Clears the screen, allowing messages to be displayed. The screen remains in this mode until the {UPDATE} command is met or the macro ends.

CURSOR
This is a variable that refers to the cell currently occupied by the cursor.

Example:
{If CURSOR=1}{LET CURSOR,2} would replace the contents of the cell occupied by the cursor with 2 if it already contained 1.

{DELAY X}
Pauses execution of the macro for X thousands of a second. This is effective only when displaying a graph or the Sheet Status screen. If X=0, execution will halt until a key is pressed.

{ESCON} and {ESCOFF}
Disables and enables the Escape key. When enabled, the Escape key allows a macro to

be aborted. Note: when using {ESCOFF}, if the macro has not been constructed properly, the computer may enter an infinite loop. In this case, the machine will need to be reset before the program can be used again.

{EXIT}
Cancels one level (or the top level if the routine is not nested) of a subroutine call. Allows users to make a forced exit from a subroutine without using a {RET} command. Can also be used to exit a loop.

{FOR COUNTER, START, STOP, STEP}
Counter = Cell location which keeps track of the number of macro iterations
Start = The beginning value for the counter
Stop = The end value for the counter
Step = The incremental value to be added to counter after each iteration

Executes the commands that follow until a {NEXT command is encountered. When this occurs, the counter is incremented by the value of "Step". When the value of "Step" is equal to or above the value specified in "Stop", the macro continues to execute from the command following the {NEXT} statement.

Notes: If "Stop" is less than "Start", the loop will be skipped. If "Step" is set to zero, an infinite loop will be created since the counter will never exceed the value in "Stop". A maximum of 4 nested loops may be used.

{GET CELL}
Accepts the next character from the keyboard and places it in "Cell". The Enter key is not needed.

{GOTOXY A1,A2}
Places the character cursor at position A1,A2 on the screen. A1 is the column (1 - 80) and A2 is the row (1 - 25). The {WRITE} command allows you to place text at the current cursor position.

{IF Condition}Action...
Tests a condition and acts according to the results of the test. If the condition is "true", the "Action" specified in the same cell will be carried out. If the condition is "false", the macro continues from the next cell down.

{INDXY m,n}
Sets the location of the Mode Indicator to line M, column N. The Mode Indicator displays program messages such as "Ready" and "Calc". The value for M must be within the range 1 - 24 and the value for N must be within the range 1 - 80.

{INKEY CELL}
Halts execution of the macro until a key is pressed, when the character used will be placed in CELL and the macro will continue.

{INLABEL "Prompt", Location}
{INVALUE "Prompt", Location}
Displays a message defined by "Prompt" and waits for input. Input may be a label (text string) or value. When Enter is pressed, the input data will be placed in cell specified by "Location".

{INRANGE "Prompt",Cell}
Displays a message defined by prompt and allows a user to mark a cell range in the normal way. The range data is then placed in the location given by "Cell".

{IOINIT "COMn:Baud,PA,DB,SB,LEN,DL"}
Initialise the serial port COMn where n=1,2,3,4.
Baud = Baud Rate (300, 1200, 2400, ...)
PA = Parity (E, O, N, ...)
DB = Data Bits (Normally 7 or 8)
SB = Stop Bits (Normally 1 or 2)
LEN = Maximum length of string that will be transmitted or accepted as input (Default is 80)
DL = Delay in units of System Cycles.

Initialises a serial port for use with the {IOVALUE} and {IOLABEL} commands.

Example:
{IOINIT "COM2:2400,N,8,1,80,2000"} initialises Port 2 for 2400 baud, no parity, 8 data bits, 1 stop bit, a maximum string length of 80 and a delay of 2000 system cycles.

{IOLABEL "String",Range}
Transmit "String" to the initialised communications port and store the received information as a label in "Range". To receive information without sending, "String" can be an empty (null) string (""). To send information without receiving, use the range name "NUL".

Example:
{IOLABEL "ATDT12345667&@CHR(13),NUL"} sends the dial up sequence ATDT1234567, followed by CR (a carriage return; Enter) to the initialised serial port. Since "Range" has been set to "NUL", no information is expected to be sent back to the computer.

{IOVALUE "String",Range}

Transmit "String" to the initialised communications port and store the received information as a label in "Range". To receive information without sending, "String" can be an empty (null) string (""). To send information without receiving, use the range name "NUL".

Example:

{IOVALUE "",A2} receives information from the other computer via the serial port and places it in A2.

{JUMP Location}

Instructs the macro to move to "Location" and continue execution from that point. "Location" can be a co-ordinate or a range name that was created with the "/RNC" command sequence. This should not be confused with {GOTO}, which simply moves the cell pointer to a new location.

{LET A1,Expression}

Evaluates "Expression" and places its value in the location specified by A1. There is no space between "," and "Expression".

{MENUCALL Location}

Transfers control to the macro menu at "Location". When the user selects an option from the menu, the macro identified is CALLed. When the new macro terminates after a {RET} command, control returns to the command following the {MENUCALL} instruction. See {MENUJUMP}.

{MENUJUMP Location}

Transfers execution to the macro menu at "Location". Users are allowed to make a menu selection that identifies a new macro to execute. Two rows are used for the menu and each menu option can be up to 30 characters long. The cell to the right of the last menu entry must be blank to indicate the end of the menu. Each selection is placed in an individual cell in the first row; the second row contains a piece of text explaining the menu item above. This text is displayed when the menu item is highlighted. A macro menu acts in the same way as a standard AsEasyAs command menu. When a menu item is selected, the program executes the macro beginning in the third row, below the chosen item.

{MENUOFF}

Disables the screen update of the panel and pop-up window menus. This speeds up the operation of macros that update the screen frequently.

{MENUON}

Restores screen update of the panel and pop-up window menus. This command should be invoked at the end of a macro that uses {MENUOFF}.

{MENUWIDTH x}
Specifies the width for a menu window (up to 28 characters). When a width is specified, it stays in effect until another {MENUWIDTH} command is encountered.

{MENUXY x,y}
Specifies the x,y position of the top left corner of a menu window. If the "." key is pressed while a menu is being displayed, the menu will toggle between the left and right sides of the screen. Although they position will remain unchanged until a new {MENUXY} command is used.

{OPEN F#,M#,"Filename"}
F# - File Number (1, 2, 3, 4, or 5)
M# - Mode (1, 2 or 3)
1 - Read - Allows the file to be read.
2 - Write - Opens a new file. If the file exists, current information will be erased.
3 - Append - Opens an existing file and places the file pointer at end of file. Filename - Name of File, may include drive and path information

Opens a disk file for read, write and append operations. A file opened with the {OPEN} command must be closed with the {CLOSE} command before exiting the program. If this is not done, the file will become corrupted.

{PICK Range,Outcell}
Range = Cell range which contains listing of labels to appear in pick list.
Outcell = Cell which will contain picked selection

Creates a pick window using the labels contained in "Range". The user may highlight a label from the list with the cursor keys. When Enter is pressed, the chosen label is placed in "Outcell"

{QUIT}
Halts execution of the macro and returns to the "Ready" mode.

{READ F#, Cell Address}
F# - File Number (1 -5)
Cell Address - Worksheet cell location (column & row) where read information is to be placed.

Reads one line at a time from File # (from the current pointer location to the next carriage return) and places the information in "Cell Address". If the end of the file is encountered, the macro will continue with the macro in the current cell or, if unsuccessful, with the macro command in the next row.

{RECALC Range}
Calculates only the specified range.

{RESTART}
Clears all levels of the subroutine stack and continues with macro execution. Within a subroutine, the {RESTART} command means that the subroutine will terminate and will not return to the calling routine.

{RET}
Returns from a subroutine to the command following the original {CALL} command that activated the subroutine. Used without a {CALL} command, an error will be generated.

{SCRNOFF}
Disables the screen update. This is used to speed up the execution of macros. The{SCRNON} and {UPDATE} commands should be used to begin updating the screen again.

{SCRNON}
Enables screen update.

{TONE A1,A2}
Generates a sound of frequency A1 (Hz) and duration A2 (milliseconds). A1 and A2 can be values, results of a calculation or cell references. This macro can also be used to cause a delay in macro execution without generating an audible tone, if desired.

{UPDATE}
Refreshes the screen.

{WHILE Test,Action}
Call the "Action" subroutine while the "Test" is true. The subroutine must have a corresponding {RET} command. When "Test" is false, the macro will continue from the command following the {WHILE} command.

{WRITE "String"}
Print "String" at the current character cursor co-ordinates. The cursor is left at the end of the printed string. This is only a temporary write. For example, if the command was used at the end of a macro, the text would be deleted immediately since the screen would be updated at the end of the macro.

{WRITE F#, "String"}
F# - File Number (1, 2, 3,...)
"String" - Information to be written to the file.

Writes "String" to the open file F#, starting from the current pointer location.

{WRITELN "String"}
Performs the same function as {WRITE}, above, but places the cursor at the beginning of the next character row.

{WRITELN F#, "String"}
Performs the same function as {WRITE}, above, but writes "String" information to the file, starting from the current pointer location, as a single line, followed by carriage return and line feed characters.

Appendix 3

Spreadsheet Functions

The functions described here are directly relevant to AsEasyAs V4. However, nearly all Lotus 1-2-3 compatible spreadsheets will provide a range of functions that are identical or at least similar to those listed here. This list covers a range of common string, mathematical, logical, financial, statistical and date functions. Advanced facilities, such as database functions, are not included.

STRING FUNCTIONS

+Co-ordinate or Value

Effectively sets the current cell equal to "value" or makes the current cell always have the same contents as "co-ordinate".

Example:
"+7" would make the current cell contain 7. If A1 contained "6*7", then +A1 would make the current cell contain "6*7", that is, 42

@@(Co-ordinate)

Indirectly addresses "co-ordinate". Note that co-ordinates should be given as strings and should use uppercase characters. If the contents of "co-ordinate" changes, the value must be refreshed by using the F9 key or the {CALC} macro command.

Example:
If A1 contains "Hello", then @@("A1") would return "Hello".

@CHR(Num)

Returns the ASCII character corresponding to Num.

Example:
@CHR(65) would return "A"

@LENGTH(String)

Returns the length of "string". Note that spaces are treated as characters.

Example:
@LENGTH("HELLO") would return 5

@MID(String,Start,Num)
Returns a section of "string", "num" characters long and starting from "start"

Example:
@MID("HELLOREADER",1,5) would return the substring "HELLO"

@N(Cell)
Returns the value contained in "cell". If the cell is blank or contains a string, zero is returned. Similar to @S

Example:
If A1 contains "17", @N(A1) would return 17

@ORD(String)
Returns the ASCII code of the first character of "string". All other characters in the string are ignored.

Example:
@ORD("ABC") would return 65

@REPEAT(String,Num)
Repeats the "string" argument "num" times.

Example:
@REPEAT("HELLO",2) would return "HELLOHELLO"

@S(Cell)
Returns the string contained in "cell". If the cell is blank or contains a value, an empty (null) string is returned. This function may be used in cases where "cell" might contain a string or a value since it does not generate an error message.

Example:
If A1 contains "Hello", @S(A1) would return "Hello"

@STR(Value,Num)
Converts "value" to a string followed by "num" digits after the decimal point.

Example:
@STR(70,3) would return "70.000"

@UPPER(String)

Converts a string so that all of the characters are upper case. Numbers and any special characters are ignored.

Example:
@UPPER("hello#~reader") would return "HELLO#~READER"

@VAL(String)

Converts a string into a numeric value. "String" may also be a string function providing a value formula is not embedded within "string". If a value formula is used, the function will return a value of zero.

Example:
@VAL("123.456") would return 123.456

MATH FUNCTIONS

Note: the arguments for all trigonometric functions must be given in radians.

@ABS(x)

Returns the absolute value of the argument.

Example:
@ABS(-23.78) would return 23.78

@ACOS(x)

Returns the arc cosine of "value" in radians.

Example:
@ACOS(0.79) would return 0.659987

@ASIN(Value)

Returns the arc sine of "value" in radians.

Example:
@ASIN(0.79) would return 0.910808

@ATAN(Value)

Returns the arc tangent of "value" in radians.

Example:

@ATAN(0.79) would return 0.668613

@COS(Value)

Returns the cosine of angle "value" in radians.

Example:
@COS(0.79) would return 0.703845

@SIN(Value)

Returns the sine of angle "value" in radians.

Example:
@SIN(0.79) would return 0.710353

@TAN Syntax: @TAN (Value)

Returns the tangent of angle "value" in radians.

Example:
@TAN(0.79) would return 1.009246

@EXP(X)

Exponential of "X". Raises "e" to the "X" power.

Example:
@EXP(12) would return 162754.7

@FALSE

Returns a value of zero. This can be used for logical operations.

Example:
If A1 contained a value above zero, @IF(A1=@FALSE,999,100) would return 100. Alternatively, if A1 were empty, a value of 999 would be returned.

@INT(Value)

Truncates "value" so that an integer is returned.

Example:
@INT(123.4567) would return 123

@LOG(Value)

Returns the base 10 logarithm of "value". Negative numbers will result in an error.

Example:
@LOG(114) would return 2.056904

@LN(Value)

Returns the natural logarithm ("base e") of "value". Negative numbers will result in an error.

Example:
@LN(114) would return 4.736198

@MOD(x,y)

Returns the remainder of "x" divided by "y": modulo division.

Example:
@MOD(29,3) would return 2

@NA

Returns a value of -1.

Example:
(27*@NA) would return -27

@PI

Returns the value of Pi: 3.1415926536

@RAND

Returns a random number.

@ROUND(x,y)

Rounds "x" to "y" decimal places. Negative numbers are rounded to the left of the decimal point.

Example:
@ROUND(123.4567,2) would return 123.46

@SQRT(Value)

Returns the square root of "value". A negative "value" will result in an error.

Example:
@SQRT(27) would return 5.196152

@TRUE
Returns a value of 1. This can be used for logical operations. See @FALSE

FINANCIAL FUNCTIONS

When using financial functions, all interest rates must be expressed as decimal fractions. Interest rates must also use the same time periods as the payment. You can produce a monthly figure by dividing the annual rate of interest by 12.

@FV(Annuity,Interest Rate,Period)
Annuity = Periodic payment amount
Interest = Periodic interest rate
Period = Number of periods

Returns the future value of an "annuity" occurring over the specified "period", using the given "interest rate".

Example:
@FV(1000, 0.12, 5) would return 635.2847 or £635.28

@IRR(Guesstimate Interest Rate,Range)
Guesstimate Interest Rate = Best guess at internal rate of return periodic interest rate
Range = Cell range which contains the cash flow return values

Returns the Rate of Return per period associated with a cash flow. The solution is iterative and may result in more than one correct answer.

Example:
If A1 contained -1000, B1 contained 500, C1 contained 500 and D1 contained 500, the formula @IRR(0.25,A1..D1) would return 0.233751 or 23.38%

@NPV(Interest Rate,Range)
Interest Rate = Periodic interest rate
Range = Cell range which in which the series of cash flows is to be stored

Returns the net present value of a cash flow over interest period.

Example:
If A1 contained 500, B1 contained 500, C1 contained 500 and D1 contained 500, the formula @NPV(0.1,A1..D1) would return 1584.932 or £1584.93

@PMT(Principal,Interest Rate,Period)

Principal = Principal amount
Interest Rate = Periodic interest rate
Period = Number of periods

Calculates the amount of an annuity equal to the principal amortised over the period.

Example:
@PMT(1000,0.1,5) would return 263.7974 or £263.80

@PV(Annuity,Interest Rate,Period)

Annuity = Periodic payment amount
Interest = Periodic interest rate
Period = Number of periods

Returns the present value corresponding to an annuity occurring over the specified period.

Example:
@PV(1000,0.1,5) would return 3790.786 or £3790.79

LOGICAL FUNCTIONS

@IF(Test,argument 1,argument 2)

Carries out a test and returns either "argument 1" or "argument 2" depending on the result of the test. "Test" can refer to the result of a cell with a logical result in it or can use logical operators including >,<,=,<>,#OR#, #AND# etc.

Example:
If A1 contains 6, @IF(A1>5,A1*10,A1*5) would return 60 ("argument 1" is used because the test is true). Alternatively, if A1 contained 4, "argument 2" would be used, giving a result of 20.

@ISNUM(Cell)

This tests the contents of "cell" and returns 1 if the cell contains a number of formula, 0 (zero) if the test is false.

Example:
If A1 contains 5, @ISNUM(A1) would return 1. If A1 contains "Hello", the function would return zero.

@ISSTR(Cell)

This tests the contents of "cell" and returns 1 if the cell contains a label or a string, 0 (zero) if the test is false.

Example:
If A1 contains "Hello", @ISSTR(A1) would return 1. If A1 contains 5, the function would return zero.

STATISTICAL FUNCTIONS

For the examples listed in this section, assume that the range A1..J1 contains the numbers 1 to 10 respectively.

@AVG(Range)

Returns the average of all values in "range".

Example:
@AVG(A1..J1) would return 5.5

@COUNT(Range)

Counts the number of elements in "range", ignoring any blank cells.

Example:
@COUNT(A1..J1) would return 10

@FACT(Value)

Returns the factorial of "value".

Example:
@FACT(7) would return 5040

@MAX(Range)

Returns the maximum value in "range".

Example:
@MAX(A1..J1) would return 10

@MIN(Range)

Returns the minimum value in "range".

Example:

@MIN(A1..J1) would return 1

@STD(Range)
Returns the standard deviation of the elements in "range".

Example:
@STD(A1..J1) would return 2.872281

@SUM(Range)
Returns the sum of all the values in "range".

Example:
@SUM(A1..J1) would return 55

@VAR(Range)
Returns the population variance of "range".

Example:
@VAR(A1..J1) would return 8.25

SPECIAL FUNCTIONS

@CASE(Number,Argument1,....Argument N)
Number = Any number or calculated value
Argument 1...Argument N = Any number, string, character

Returns the argument corresponding to its "number" in the list.

Example:
@CASE(3,"A","B","C",1,2,3) would return "C"

@COLS(Range)
Returns the number of columns in "range"

Example:
@COLS(A1..J1) would return 10

@HTABLE(Criterion,Range,Offset)
Criterion = Value to be used for match in top row of range
Range = Cell range which contains criterion range as top row and includes data value table

Offset = Number of rows down in data value table from which to return a value

Returns the value at a vertical offset in the column that matches the criterion. The first row of the range contains the values that the @HTABLE function will search for a match with the "criterion". Once the closest match has been found, the function returns the value "offset" rows down.

Example:
Assuming that the range A2..J2 contains the values from 100 to 1000, using increments of 100, @HTABLE(7,A1..J2,1) would return 700.

@HTERP(Cell,Range,Offset)

Performs a straight-line interpolation based on table specified by "range". It operates similar to @HTABLE function, but returns an interpolated value rather than a value in the table.

Example:
Assuming that the range A2..J2 contains the values from 100 to 1000, using increments of 100, and that A5 contains the value 5.5, @HTERP(A5,A1..J2,1) would return 550.

@LINK("Filename>Cell")

This links the current cell to "cell" in a worksheet on disk. The double quotes and the ">" are character are necessary. When this function is used, it often returns an error message since the link has not yet been updated. This can be overcome by selecting "Uplink" from the "File" sub-menu. When this is done, the program retrieves the data from the worksheet on disk and places it in the linked cell. Note that the data in the worksheet on disk is relatively static: it will not be updated prior to being extracted for use in the current worksheet.

Example:
Assuming that A1 in "EXAMPLE.WKS" contains 1000, @LINK ("EXAMPLE.WKS>A1") would place 1000 in the current cell (after the link had been updated).

@ROWS(Range)

Returns the number of rows in "range".

Example:
@ROWS(A1..J1) would return 1

@VTABLE(Criterion,Range,Offset)

Criterion = Value to be used for match in left column of range

Range = Cell range which contains criterion range as left column and includes data value table
Offset = Number of columns right in data value table from which to return a value

Returns the value at a horizontal offset in the row that matches the criterion. This operates in much the same way as the @HTABLE function.

Example:
Assuming that A1 contained 1, A2 contained 2, A3 contained 3, B1 contained 100, B2 contained 200 and B3 contained 300, then @VTABLE(2,A1..B3,1) would return 200

@VTERP(Cell,Range,Offset)
Similar to @HTERP, but scans vertically (row by row).

Example:
Assuming that A1 contained 1, A2 contained 2, A3 contained 3, B1 contained 100, B2 contained 200, B3 contained 300 and A5 contained 1.2, then @HTERP(A5, A1..B3,1) would return 2.4

DATE AND TIME FUNCTIONS

The date functions are based on the number of days since 1 January1900. To display values in date form, the cell should be formatted with one of the date formats (see 4.11).

@DATE(Year,Month,Day)
Year = Value corresponding to last two digits of year
Month = Value corresponding to month of year, 1-12
Day = Value corresponding to day of month, 1-31

Returns a unique number for each day since 1 January 1900.

Example:
@DATE(66,1,15) would return 24122 (15 January 1966).

@DATEVAL("MM/DD/YY")
Converts a string argument to a number representing a month, day and year. Note that the cell can be formatted to display the value as a date.

Example:
@DATEVAL("1/15/66") would return 24122. However, if the cell had been formatted

as a date, it would be shown as "15-Jan-66".

@DAY(Value)

Based on a unique day assigned to "value", the day in the month for that date is returned.

Example:
@DAY(24122) would return 15 (as in 15 January 1966)

@HOUR(Value)

Returns the hours corresponding the fractional portion of "value". The integer portion of "value", which represents days, is ignored.

Example:
@HOUR(4.25) would return 6

@MINUTE(Value)

Returns the minutes corresponding to the fractional portion of "value". The integer portion of "value", which represents days, is ignored.

Example:
@MINUTE(4.26) would return 14

@MONTH(Value)

Based on a unique day assigned to "value", the month in which that day occurs is returned.

Example:
@MONTH(24122) would return 1 (as in 15 January 1966)

@SECOND(Value)

Returns the seconds corresponding to the fractional portion of "value". The integer portion of "value", which represents days, is ignored.

Example:
@SECOND(4.26) would return 24

@TIMEVAL("HH:MM:SS")

HH = Value representing number of hours
MM = Value representing number of minutes
SS = Value representing number of seconds

Converts a string into a real number representing the hours, minutes and seconds as a fraction of a day. The cell can be formatted to display the value in a time format. The time value is calculated using the following formula:

$$\frac{\text{HOUR} + (\text{MINUTES}/60) + (\text{SECONDS}/3600)}{24}$$

Example:
@TIMEVAL("12:15:00") would return 0.510416. However, if the cell had been formatted as a time, "12:15:00pm" would be displayed.

@TODAY

Returns a unique number corresponding to today's date. The number is derived from a starting point set at 1 January 1900. The @TODAY function is not automatically updated when a spreadsheet is retrieved from disk: it must be updated by manually recalculating the worksheet via the F9 key or {CALC} macro command.

Example:
@TODAY returns the number 33907 if today is 30th October 1992. If the cell had been formatted as a date, "30-Oct-92" would be displayed.

@YEAR(Value)

Based on a unique day assigned to "value", the year in which that day occurs is returned.

Example:
@YEAR(24122) returns 66 (as in 15 January 1966)

Appendix 4

Worksheet Exercises

The blank cells in some listings have been retained deliberately in order to make each listing mre legible.

I. Car Expenses

```
B1 [W16]: ^Car Expenses
C1: '>This line centred
B2 [W16]: ^————
C2: '>This line centred
A4: 'Road Tax
B4 [C2 W16]: 100
C4: '>Formatted as currency
A5: 'Insurance
B5 [C2 W16]: 150
A6: 'MOT
B6 [C2 W16]: 75
A7: 'Services
B7 [C2 W16]: 150
A8: 'Repairs
B8 [C2 W16]: 225
A9: 'Fuel
B9 [C2 W16]: 62.5*12
A10: \-
B10 [C2 W16]: \-
C10: '>This line 'filled'
A11: 'Total:
B11 [C2 W16]: @SUM(B4..B9)
C11: '>Contains formula @SUM(B4..B9)
A12: \=
B12 [W16]: \=
C12: '>This line 'filled'
B14 [W16]: 'Column width increased to 16
```

II. Random Numbers, Graphs And Macro Example

```
A1 [W15]: 'GRAPH AND MACRO EXAMPLE
D1: '
A2 [W15]: '======================
B4: ^ONE
C4: ^TWO
D4: ^THREE
E4: ^FOUR
F4: ^FIVE
G4: ^SIX
H4: ^SEVEN
I4: ^EIGHT
J4: ^NINE
K4: ^TEN
A5 [W15]: \-
B5: \-
C5: \-
D5: \-
E5: \-
F5: \-
G5: \-
H5: \-
I5: \-
J5: \-
K5: \-
A6 [W15]: 'X RANDOM DATA
B6: @INT(@RAND*100)+1
C6: @INT(@RAND*100)+1
D6: @INT(@RAND*100)+1
E6: @INT(@RAND*100)+1
F6: @INT(@RAND*100)+1
G6: @INT(@RAND*100)+1
H6: @INT(@RAND*100)+1
I6: @INT(@RAND*100)+1
J6: @INT(@RAND*100)+1
K6: @INT(@RAND*100)+1
A7 [W15]: \-
B7: \-
C7: \-
D7: \-
E7: \-
F7: \-
G7: \-
```

```
H7: \-
I7: \-
J7: \-
K7: \-
A8 [W15]: 'Y RANDOM DATA
B8: @INT(@RAND*100)+1
C8: @INT(@RAND*100)+1
D8: @INT(@RAND*100)+1
E8: @INT(@RAND*100)+1
F8: @INT(@RAND*100)+1
G8: @INT(@RAND*100)+1
H8: @INT(@RAND*100)+1
I8: @INT(@RAND*100)+1
J8: @INT(@RAND*100)+1
K8: @INT(@RAND*100)+1
A9 [W15]: \-
B9: \-
C9: \-
D9: \-
E9: \-
F9: \-
G9: \-
H9: \-
I9: \-
J9: \-
K9: \-
A10 [W15]: 'Y1 RANDOM DATA
B10: @INT(@RAND*100)+1
C10: @INT(@RAND*100)+1
D10: @INT(@RAND*100)+1
E10: @INT(@RAND*100)+1
F10: @INT(@RAND*100)+1
G10: @INT(@RAND*100)+1
H10: @INT(@RAND*100)+1
I10: @INT(@RAND*100)+1
J10: @INT(@RAND*100)+1
K10: @INT(@RAND*100)+1
A11 [W15]: \-
B11: \-
C11: \-
D11: \-
E11: \-
F11: \-
G11: \-
H11: \-
I11: \-
J11: \-
```

```
K11: \-
A14 [W15]: 'VIEW GRAPHS MACRO [ALT-G]
A15 [W15]: '========================
D15: '
A17 [W15]: '/gxb6..k6~
D17: 'SET X RANGE
A18 [W15]: 'ab8..k8~
D18: 'SET Y RANGE
A19 [W15]: 'bb10..k10~
D19: 'SET Y1 RANGE
A20 [W15]: 'otf{del 20}Test~{esc 5}
D20: 'SET MAIN TITLE
A21 [W15]: '/gots{del 20}Random Data~{esc 5}
D21: 'SET 2ND TITLE
A22 [W15]: '/gotx{del 20}X Axis~{esc 5}
D22: 'SET X AXIS TITLE
A23 [W15]: '/goty{del 20}Y Axis~{esc 5}
D23: 'SET Y AXIS TITLE
A24 [W15]: '/gosys4~qqq
D24: 'SET VERTICAL SCALE
A25 [W15]: 'ogbq
D25: 'SET GRID ON
A26 [W15]: 'tbv
D26: 'VIEW BAR GRAPH
A27 [W15]: 'tpv
D27: 'VIEW PIE CHART
A28 [W15]: 'tav{esc}
D28: 'VIEW AREA GRAPH
```

III. Basic Cashflow Exercise

```
A1 [W16]: 'MEGAWIDGET INTERNATIONAL - BASIC CASHFLOW FORECAST
A2 [W16]:
A3 [W16]: 'The following spreadsheet models the finances for
Megawidget
A4 [W16]: 'International for the period January 1993 - December
1993.
A5 [W16]:
A6 [W16]: 'The cashflow forecast is located at A21. (Macro ALT-C)
A7 [W16]:
A8 [W16]: 'Starting values are located at A61. (Macro ALT-S)
A9 [W16]:
A10 [W16]: 'Macros are located at A81. (Macro ALT-M)
A11 [W16]:
```

```
A18 [W16]: 'Compiled by Paul Bocij, Director of Finances
A19 [W16]:
A20 [W16]: 'Press PAGE DOWN to view cashflow forecast.

A21 [W16]: 'MEGAWIDGET INTERNATIONAL - BASIC CASHFLOW FORECAST
C23 [W13]: ^JAN
D23 [W13]: ^FEB
E23 [W13]: ^MARCH
F23 [W13]: ^APRIL
G23 [W13]: ^MAY
H23 [W13]: ^JUNE
I23 [W13]: ^JULY
J23 [W13]: ^AUGUST
K23 [W13]: ^SEPT
L23 [W13]: ^OCT
M23 [W13]: ^NOV
N23 [W13]: ^DEC
P23 [W12]: ^SUBTOTAL
C24 [W13]: \=
D24 [W13]: \=
E24 [W13]: \=
F24 [W13]: \=
G24 [W13]: \=
H24 [W13]: \=
I24 [W13]: \=
J24 [W13]: \=
K24 [W13]: \=
L24 [W13]: \=
M24 [W13]: \=
N24 [W13]: \=
P24 [W12]: ^========
A25 [W16]: 'CASH INFLOWS
A26 [W16]: \-
A27 [W16]: 'SALES (UNITS)
C27 [F0 W13]: (C64)
D27 [F0 W13]: (C27*(1+$E$65))
E27 [F0 W13]: (D27*(1+$E$65))
F27 [F0 W13]: (E27*(1+$E$65))
G27 [F0 W13]: (F27*(1+$E$65))
H27 [F0 W13]: (G27*(1+$E$65))
I27 [F0 W13]: (H27*(1+$E$65))
J27 [F0 W13]: (I27*(1+$E$65))
K27 [F0 W13]: (J27*(1+$E$65))
L27 [F0 W13]: (K27*(1+$E$65))
M27 [F0 W13]: (L27*(1+$E$65))
N27 [F0 W13]: (M27*(1+$E$65))
O27 [C2]:
```

```
P27 [F0 W12]: @SUM(C27..N27)
A28 [W16]: 'SALES
C28 [C2 W13]: (C64*C63)
D28 [C2 W13]: (D27*$C$63)
E28 [C2 W13]: (E27*$C$63)
F28 [C2 W13]: (F27*$C$63)
G28 [C2 W13]: (G27*$C$63)
H28 [C2 W13]: (H27*$C$63)
I28 [C2 W13]: (I27*$C$63)
J28 [C2 W13]: (J27*$C$63)
K28 [C2 W13]: (K27*$C$63)
L28 [C2 W13]: (L27*$C$63)
M28 [C2 W13]: (M27*$C$63)
N28 [C2 W13]: (N27*$C$63)
O28 [C2]:
P28 [C2 W12]: @SUM(C28..N28)
A29 [W16]: 'INTEREST
C29 [C2 W13]: ($E$72*$C$70)
D29 [C2 W13]: ($E$72*$C$70)
E29 [C2 W13]: ($E$72*$C$70)
F29 [C2 W13]: ($E$72*$C$70)
G29 [C2 W13]: ($E$72*$C$70)
H29 [C2 W13]: ($E$72*$C$70)
I29 [C2 W13]: ($E$72*$C$70)
J29 [C2 W13]: ($E$72*$C$70)
K29 [C2 W13]: ($E$72*$C$70)
L29 [C2 W13]: ($E$72*$C$70)
M29 [C2 W13]: ($E$72*$C$70)
N29 [C2 W13]: ($E$72*$C$70)
O29 [C2]:
P29 [C2 W12]: @SUM(C29..N29)
A30 [W16]: \-
B30: \-
C30 [C2 W13]: \-
D30 [C2 W13]: \-
E30 [C2 W13]: \-
F30 [C2 W13]: \-
G30 [C2 W13]: \-
H30 [C2 W13]: \-
I30 [C2 W13]: \-
J30 [C2 W13]: \-
K30 [C2 W13]: \-
L30 [C2 W13]: \-
M30 [C2 W13]: \-
N30 [C2 W13]: \-
O30 [C2]:
P30 [C2 W12]:
```

```
A31 [W16]: 'SUBTOTAL
C31 [C2 W13]: @SUM(C28..C29)
D31 [C2 W13]: @SUM(D28..D29)
E31 [C2 W13]: @SUM(E28..E29)
F31 [C2 W13]: @SUM(F28..F29)
G31 [C2 W13]: @SUM(G28..G29)
H31 [C2 W13]: @SUM(H28..H29)
I31 [C2 W13]: @SUM(I28..I29)
J31 [C2 W13]: @SUM(J28..J29)
K31 [C2 W13]: @SUM(K28..K29)
L31 [C2 W13]: @SUM(L28..L29)
M31 [C2 W13]: @SUM(M28..M29)
N31 [C2 W13]: @SUM(N28..N29)
O31 [C2]:
P31 [C2 W12]: @SUM(C31..N31)
A32 [W16]: \-
B32: \-
C32 [C2 W13]: \-
D32 [C2 W13]: \-
E32 [C2 W13]: \-
F32 [C2 W13]: \-
G32 [C2 W13]: \-
H32 [C2 W13]: \-
I32 [C2 W13]: \-
J32 [C2 W13]: \-
K32 [C2 W13]: \-
L32 [C2 W13]: \-
M32 [C2 W13]: \-
N32 [C2 W13]: \-
O32 [C2]:
P32 [C2 W12]:
O33 [C2]:
P33 [C2 W12]:
A34 [W16]: 'CASH OUTFLOWS
C34 [C2 W13]:
O34 [C2]:
P34 [C2 W12]:
A35 [W16]: \-
C35 [C2 W13]:
O35 [C2]:
P35 [C2 W12]:
A36 [W16]: 'MATERIALS
C36 [C2 W13]: (C27*$C$66)
D36 [C2 W13]: (D27*$C$66)
E36 [C2 W13]: (E27*$C$66)
F36 [C2 W13]: (F27*$C$66)
G36 [C2 W13]: (G27*$C$66)
```

```
H36 [C2 W13]: (H27*$C$66)
I36 [C2 W13]: (I27*$C$66)
J36 [C2 W13]: (J27*$C$66)
K36 [C2 W13]: (K27*$C$66)
L36 [C2 W13]: (L27*$C$66)
M36 [C2 W13]: (M27*$C$66)
N36 [C2 W13]: (N27*$C$66)
O36 [C2]:
P36 [C2 W12]: @SUM(C36..N36)
A37 [W16]: 'LABOUR
C37 [C2 W13]: (C27*$C$67)
D37 [C2 W13]: (D27*$C$67)
E37 [C2 W13]: (E27*$C$67)
F37 [C2 W13]: (F27*$C$67)
G37 [C2 W13]: (G27*$C$67)
H37 [C2 W13]: (H27*$C$67)
I37 [C2 W13]: (I27*$C$67)
J37 [C2 W13]: (J27*$C$67)
K37 [C2 W13]: (K27*$C$67)
L37 [C2 W13]: (L27*$C$67)
M37 [C2 W13]: (M27*$C$67)
N37 [C2 W13]: (N27*$C$67)
O37 [C2]:
P37 [C2 W12]: @SUM(C37..N37)
A38 [W16]: 'POWER,LIGHT,HEAT
C38 [C2 W13]: (C27*$C$68)
D38 [C2 W13]: (D27*$C$68)
E38 [C2 W13]: (E27*$C$68)
F38 [C2 W13]: (F27*$C$68)
G38 [C2 W13]: (G27*$C$68)
H38 [C2 W13]: (H27*$C$68)
I38 [C2 W13]: (I27*$C$68)
J38 [C2 W13]: (J27*$C$68)
K38 [C2 W13]: (K27*$C$68)
L38 [C2 W13]: (L27*$C$68)
M38 [C2 W13]: (M27*$C$68)
N38 [C2 W13]: (N27*$C$68)
O38 [C2]:
P38 [C2 W12]: @SUM(C38..N38)
A39 [W16]: 'PREMISES
C39 [C2 W13]: ($C$69)
D39 [C2 W13]: ($C$69)
E39 [C2 W13]: ($C$69)
F39 [C2 W13]: ($C$69)
G39 [C2 W13]: ($C$69)
H39 [C2 W13]: ($C$69)
I39 [C2 W13]: ($C$69)
```

```
J39 [C2 W13]: ($C$69)
K39 [C2 W13]: ($C$69)
L39 [C2 W13]: ($C$69)
M39 [C2 W13]: ($C$69)
N39 [C2 W13]: ($C$69)
O39 [C2]:
P39 [C2 W12]: @SUM(C39..N39)
A40 [W16]: \-
B40: \-
C40 [W13]: \-
D40 [W13]: \-
E40 [W13]: \-
F40 [W13]: \-
G40 [C2 W13]: \-
H40 [W13]: \-
I40 [W13]: \-
J40 [W13]: \-
K40 [W13]: \-
L40 [W13]: \-
M40 [W13]: \-
N40 [W13]: \-
A41 [W16]: 'SUBTOTAL
C41 [C2 W13]: @SUM(C36..C39)
D41 [C2 W13]: @SUM(D36..D39)
E41 [C2 W13]: @SUM(E36..E39)
F41 [C2 W13]: @SUM(F36..F39)
G41 [C2 W13]: @SUM(G36..G39)
H41 [C2 W13]: @SUM(H36..H39)
I41 [C2 W13]: @SUM(I36..I39)
J41 [C2 W13]: @SUM(J36..J39)
K41 [C2 W13]: @SUM(K36..K39)
L41 [C2 W13]: @SUM(L36..L39)
M41 [C2 W13]: @SUM(M36..M39)
N41 [C2 W13]: @SUM(N36..N39)
P41 [C2 W12]: @SUM(C41..N41)
A42 [W16]: \-
B42: \-
C42 [W13]: \-
D42 [W13]: \-
E42 [W13]: \-
F42 [W13]: \-
G42 [W13]: \-
H42 [W13]: \-
I42 [W13]: \-
J42 [W13]: \-
K42 [W13]: \-
L42 [W13]: \-
```

```
M42 [W13]: \-
N42 [W13]: \-
C43 [C2 W13]:
P43 [C2 W12]:
A44 [W16]: \=
B44: \=
C44 [C2 W13]: \=
D44 [C2 W13]: \=
E44 [C2 W13]: \=
F44 [C2 W13]: \=
G44 [C2 W13]: \=
H44 [C2 W13]: \=
I44 [C2 W13]: \=
J44 [C2 W13]: \=
K44 [C2 W13]: \=
L44 [C2 W13]: \=
M44 [C2 W13]: \=
N44 [C2 W13]: \=
O44 [C2]:
P44 [C2 W12]:
A45 [W16]: 'MONTHLY BALANCE
C45 [C2 W13]: (C31-C41)
D45 [C2 W13]: (C45+D31-D41)
E45 [C2 W13]: (D45+E31-E41)
F45 [C2 W13]: (E45+F31-F41)
G45 [C2 W13]: (F45+G31-G41)
H45 [C2 W13]: (G45+H31-H41)
I45 [C2 W13]: (H45+I31-I41)
J45 [C2 W13]: (I45+J31-J41)
K45 [C2 W13]: (J45+K31-K41)
L45 [C2 W13]: (K45+L31-L41)
M45 [C2 W13]: (L45+M31-M41)
N45 [C2 W13]: (M45+N31-N41)
O45 [C2]:
P45 [C2 W12]:
A46 [W16]: \=
B46: \=
C46 [C2 W13]: \=
D46 [C2 W13]: \=
E46 [C2 W13]: \=
F46 [C2 W13]: \=
G46 [C2 W13]: \=
H46 [C2 W13]: \=
I46 [C2 W13]: \=
J46 [C2 W13]: \=
K46 [C2 W13]: \=
L46 [C2 W13]: \=
```

```
M46 [C2 W13]: \=
N46 [C2 W13]: \=
O46 [C2]:
O48 [C2]:
P48 [C2 W12]:
A61 [W16]: 'STARTING VALUES FOR MEGAWIDGET CASHFLOW FORECAST
A62 [W16]:
A63 [W16]: 'SELLING PRICE
C63 [W13]: 9.99
D63 [W13]:
A64 [W16]: 'STARTING SALES
C64 [W13]: 1000
D64 [W13]: 'UNITS
A65 [W16]: 'SALES GROWTH P.M.
C65 [W13]: 5
D65 [W13]: '% GIVING
E65 [W13]: (C65/100)
A66 [W16]: 'MATERIALS COST P.U.
C66 [W13]: 5.75
D66 [W13]:
A67 [W16]: 'LABOUR COST P.U.
C67 [W13]: 1.23
D67 [W13]:
A68 [W16]: 'POWER COST P.U.
C68 [W13]: 0.77
D68 [W13]:
A69 [W16]: 'MONTHLY RENTAL
C69 [W13]: 3000
D69 [W13]:
A70 [W16]: 'SAVINGS ACCOUNT
C70 [W13]: 25000
D70 [W13]:
A71 [W16]: 'INTEREST RATE P.A.
C71 [W13]: 12
D71 [W13]: '% - OR
E71 [W13]: (C71/12)
F71 [W13]: '% PER MONTH
D72 [W13]: '  - GIVING
E72 [W13]: (E71/100)
A81 [W16]: 'MACROS
A82 [W16]: '======
A84 [W16]: '{goto}a21~
B84: 'ALT-C: GOTO CASHFLOW FORECAST
A86 [W16]: '{goto}a61~
B86: 'ALT-S: GOTO STARTING VALUES
A88 [W16]: '{goto}a81~
B88: 'ALT-M: GOTO MACROS
```

IV. Advanced Financial Modelling Exercise

```
A1: 'MEGAWIDGET INTERNATIONAL - CASHFLOW FORECAST
AA1: 'MEGAWIDGET INTERNATIONAL - CASHFLOW FORECAST
BD1 [W12]: 'DATA ENTRY SCREEN
CA1 [W12]: 'REPORT AREA
A2: '==========================================
AA2: '==========================================
BD2 [W12]: '================
CA2 [W12]: '===========
AC3 [W13]: ^JAN
AD3 [W13]: ^FEB
AE3 [W13]: ^MARCH
AF3 [W13]: ^APRIL
AG3 [W13]: ^MAY
AH3 [W13]: ^JUNE
AI3 [W13]: ^JULY
AJ3 [W13]: ^AUGUST
AK3 [W13]: ^SEPT
AL3 [W13]: ^OCT
AM3 [W13]: ^NOV
AN3 [W13]: ^DEC
AP3 [W13]: ^SUBTOTAL
BA3: 'SELLING PRICE:
BD3 [C2 W12]: 10.05
BF3 [W12]: 'AVERAGE E.O.Y.
A4: 'This model represents the cashflow forecast for MegaWidget
International
AC4 [W13]: \=
AD4 [W13]: \=
AE4 [W13]: \=
AF4 [W13]: \=
AG4 [W13]: \=
AH4 [W13]: \=
AI4 [W13]: \=
AJ4 [W13]: \=
AK4 [W13]: \=
AL4 [W13]: \=
AM4 [W13]: \=
AN4 [W13]: \=
AP4 [W13]: ^========
BA4: 'STARTING SALES:
BD4 [W12]: 1100
BF4 [W12]: '   BALANCE
CA4 [W12]: ^STARTING
CB4 [W12]: ^SELLING
```

```
CC4 [W12]: ^MATERIALS
CD4 [W12]: ^LABOUR
CE4 [W12]: ^POWER
CF4 [W12]: ^INVESTMENT
CG4 [W12]: ^INTEREST
CH4 [W12]: ^TOTAL
CI4 [W12]: ^TOTAL
CJ4 [W12]: ^E.O.Y.
CK4 [W12]: ^AVERAGE
A5: 'for the period January 1993 - December 1993.
AA5: 'CASH INFLOWS
BA5: 'MATERIALS COST:
BD5 [C2 W12]: 5.75
CA5 [W12]: ^SALES
CB5 [W12]: ^PRICE
CG5 [W12]: ^RATE
CH5 [W12]: ^SALES ( )
CI5 [W12]: ^EXPENSES
CJ5 [W12]: ^BALANCE
CK5 [W12]: ^E.O.Y. BAL
AA6: \-
BA6: 'LABOUR COST:
BD6 [C2 W12]: 1.23
BF6 [C2 W12]: 3423.37242
CA6 [W12]: \-
CB6 [W12]: \-
CC6 [W12]: \-
CD6 [W12]: \-
CE6 [W12]: \-
CF6 [W12]: \-
CG6 [W12]: \-
CH6 [W12]: \-
CI6 [W12]: \-
CJ6 [W12]: \-
CK6 [W12]: \-
A7: 'This model constructed by Paul Bocij, Director of Financial
Planning
AA7: 'SALES (UNITS)
AC7 [F0 W13]: +C153
AD7 [F0 W13]: (AC7*(1+(C117/100)))
AE7 [F0 W13]: (AD7*(1+(D117/100)))
AF7 [F0 W13]: (AE7*(1+(E117/100)))
AG7 [F0 W13]: (AF7*(1+(F117/100)))
AH7 [F0 W13]: (AG7*(1+(G117/100)))
AI7 [F0 W13]: (AH7*(1+(H117/100)))
AJ7 [F0 W13]: (AI7*(1+(I117/100)))
AK7 [F0 W13]: (AJ7*(1+(J117/100)))
```

```
AL7 [F0 W13]: (AK7*(1+(K117/100)))
AM7 [F0 W13]: (AL7*(1+(L117/100)))
AN7 [F0 W13]: (AM7*(1+(M117/100)))
AO7 [C2]:
AP7 [F0 W13]: @SUM(AC7..AN7)
AQ7 [C2]:
BA7: 'POWER COST:
BD7 [C2 W12]: 0.77
BF7 [W12]:
BZ7: '1.
CB7 [C2 W12]:
CJ7 [C2 W12]:
CK7 [C2 W12]:
AA8: 'SALES (£)
AC8 [C2 W13]: (AC7*$C$152)
AD8 [C2 W13]: (AD7*$C$152)
AE8 [C2 W13]: (AE7*$C$152)
AF8 [C2 W13]: (AF7*$C$152)
AG8 [C2 W13]: (AG7*$C$152)
AH8 [C2 W13]: (AH7*$C$152)
AI8 [C2 W13]: (AI7*$C$152)
AJ8 [C2 W13]: (AJ7*$C$152)
AK8 [C2 W13]: (AK7*$C$152)
AL8 [C2 W13]: (AL7*$C$152)
AM8 [C2 W13]: (AM7*$C$152)
AN8 [C2 W13]: (AN7*$C$152)
AO8 [C2]:
AP8 [C2 W13]: @SUM(AC8..AN8)
AQ8 [C2]:
BA8: 'INVESTMENT:
BD8 [C2 W12]: 25000
BF8 [W12]:
BZ8: '2.
CB8 [C2 W12]:
CK8 [C2 W12]:
A9: 'The cashflow forecast is stored at AA1 (ALT-C)
AA9: 'INTEREST
AC9 [C2 W13]: ($E$161*$C$159)
AD9 [C2 W13]: ($E$161*$C$159)
AE9 [C2 W13]: ($E$161*$C$159)
AF9 [C2 W13]: ($E$161*$C$159)
AG9 [C2 W13]: ($E$161*$C$159)
AH9 [C2 W13]: ($E$161*$C$159)
AI9 [C2 W13]: ($E$161*$C$159)
AJ9 [C2 W13]: ($E$161*$C$159)
AK9 [C2 W13]: ($E$161*$C$159)
AL9 [C2 W13]: ($E$161*$C$159)
```

```
AM9 [C2 W13]: ($E$161*$C$159)
AN9 [C2 W13]: ($E$161*$C$159)
AO9 [C2]:
AP9 [C2 W13]: @SUM(AC9..AN9)
AQ9 [C2]:
BA9: 'INTEREST RATE:
BD9 [F2 W12]: 12
BZ9: '3.
CB9 [C2 W12]:
CK9 [C2 W12]:
A10: 'The macro data is stored at A50 (ALT-K)
AA10: \-
AB10: \-
AC10 [C2 W13]: \-
AD10 [C2 W13]: \-
AE10 [C2 W13]: \-
AF10 [C2 W13]: \-
AG10 [C2 W13]: \-
AH10 [C2 W13]: \-
AI10 [C2 W13]: \-
AJ10 [C2 W13]: \-
AK10 [C2 W13]: \-
AL10 [C2 W13]: \-
AM10 [C2 W13]: \-
AN10 [C2 W13]: \-
AO10 [C2]:
AP10 [C2 W13]:
AQ10 [C2]:
BZ10: '4.
CB10 [C2 W12]:
CK10 [C2 W12]:
A11: 'The default data is stored at A150 (ALT-D)*   See Note
AA11: 'SUBTOTAL
AC11 [C2 W13]: @SUM(AC8..AC9)
AD11 [C2 W13]: @SUM(AD8..AD9)
AE11 [C2 W13]: @SUM(AE8..AE9)
AF11 [C2 W13]: @SUM(AF8..AF9)
AG11 [C2 W13]: @SUM(AG8..AG9)
AH11 [C2 W13]: @SUM(AH8..AH9)
AI11 [C2 W13]: @SUM(AI8..AI9)
AJ11 [C2 W13]: @SUM(AJ8..AJ9)
AK11 [C2 W13]: @SUM(AK8..AK9)
AL11 [C2 W13]: @SUM(AL8..AL9)
AM11 [C2 W13]: @SUM(AM8..AM9)
AN11 [C2 W13]: @SUM(AN8..AN9)
AO11 [C2]:
AP11 [C2 W13]: @SUM(AC11..AN11)
```

```
AQ11 [C2]:
BA11: \-
BB11: \-
BC11: \-
BD11 [W12]: \-
BE11: \-
BF11 [W12]: \-
BZ11: '5.
CB11 [C2 W12]:
CK11 [C2 W12]:
A12: 'The Monte Carlo Analysis data is stored at A100 (ALT-M)
AA12: \-
AB12: \-
AC12 [C2 W13]: \-
AD12 [C2 W13]: \-
AE12 [C2 W13]: \-
AF12 [C2 W13]: \-
AG12 [C2 W13]: \-
AH12 [C2 W13]: \-
AI12 [C2 W13]: \-
AJ12 [C2 W13]: \-
AK12 [C2 W13]: \-
AL12 [C2 W13]: \-
AM12 [C2 W13]: \-
AN12 [C2 W13]: \-
AO12 [C2]:
AP12 [C2 W13]:
AQ12 [C2]:
BZ12: '6.
CB12 [C2 W12]:
CK12 [C2 W12]:
A13: 'The results screen is stored at BA1 (ALT-E)
AC13 [C2 W13]:
AN13 [C2 W13]:
AO13 [C2]:
AP13 [C2 W13]:
AQ13 [C2]:
BA13: 'TOTAL SALES (UNITS):
BF13 [F0 W12]: +AP7
BZ13: '7.
CB13 [C2 W12]:
CK13 [C2 W12]:
A14: 'The report area is located at CA1 (ALT-P)
AA14: 'CASH OUTFLOWS
AC14 [C2 W13]:
AN14 [C2 W13]:
AO14 [C2]:
```

```
AP14 [C2 W13]:
AQ14 [C2]:
BA14: 'TOTAL SALES ( ):
BF14 [C2 W12]: +AP8
BZ14: '8.
CB14 [C2 W12]:
CK14 [C2 W12]:
AA15: \-
AC15 [C2 W13]:
AN15 [C2 W13]:
AO15 [C2]:
AP15 [C2 W13]:
AQ15 [C2]:
BA15: 'TOTAL EXPENSES:
BF15 [C2 W12]: +AP21
BZ15: '9.
CB15 [C2 W12]:
CK15 [C2 W12]:
AA16: 'MATERIALS
AC16 [C2 W13]: (AC7*$C$155)
AD16 [C2 W13]: (AD7*$C$155)
AE16 [C2 W13]: (AE7*$C$155)
AF16 [C2 W13]: (AF7*$C$155)
AG16 [C2 W13]: (AG7*$C$155)
AH16 [C2 W13]: (AH7*$C$155)
AI16 [C2 W13]: (AI7*$C$155)
AJ16 [C2 W13]: (AJ7*$C$155)
AK16 [C2 W13]: (AK7*$C$155)
AL16 [C2 W13]: (AL7*$C$155)
AM16 [C2 W13]: (AM7*$C$155)
AN16 [C2 W13]: (AN7*$C$155)
AO16 [C2]:
AP16 [C2 W13]: @SUM(AC16..AN16)
AQ16 [C2]:
BA16: 'E.O.Y. BALANCE:
BF16 [C2 W12]: +AN25
BZ16: '10.
CB16 [C2 W12]:
CK16 [C2 W12]:
AA17: 'LABOUR
AC17 [C2 W13]: (AC7*$C$156)
AD17 [C2 W13]: (AD7*$C$156)
AE17 [C2 W13]: (AE7*$C$156)
AF17 [C2 W13]: (AF7*$C$156)
AG17 [C2 W13]: (AG7*$C$156)
AH17 [C2 W13]: (AH7*$C$156)
AI17 [C2 W13]: (AI7*$C$156)
```

```
AJ17 [C2 W13]: (AJ7*$C$156)
AK17 [C2 W13]: (AK7*$C$156)
AL17 [C2 W13]: (AL7*$C$156)
AM17 [C2 W13]: (AM7*$C$156)
AN17 [C2 W13]: (AN7*$C$156)
AO17 [C2]:
AP17 [C2 W13]: @SUM(AC17..AN17)
AQ17 [C2]:
BA17: \-
BB17: \-
BC17: \-
BD17 [W12]: \-
BE17: \-
BF17 [W12]: \-
BZ17: '11.
CB17 [C2 W12]:
CK17 [C2 W12]:
AA18: 'POWER,LIGHT,HEAT
AC18 [C2 W13]: (AC7*$C$157)
AD18 [C2 W13]: (AD7*$C$157)
AE18 [C2 W13]: (AE7*$C$157)
AF18 [C2 W13]: (AF7*$C$157)
AG18 [C2 W13]: (AG7*$C$157)
AH18 [C2 W13]: (AH7*$C$157)
AI18 [C2 W13]: (AI7*$C$157)
AJ18 [C2 W13]: (AJ7*$C$157)
AK18 [C2 W13]: (AK7*$C$157)
AL18 [C2 W13]: (AL7*$C$157)
AM18 [C2 W13]: (AM7*$C$157)
AN18 [C2 W13]: (AN7*$C$157)
AO18 [C2]:
AP18 [C2 W13]: @SUM(AC18..AN18)
AQ18 [C2]:
BA18: 'Press ALT-R to restore default data
BZ18: '12.
CB18 [C2 W12]:
CK18 [C2 W12]:
AA19: 'PREMISES
AC19 [C2 W13]: +($C$158)
AD19 [C2 W13]: +($C$158)
AE19 [C2 W13]: +($C$158)
AF19 [C2 W13]: +($C$158)
AG19 [C2 W13]: +($C$158)
AH19 [C2 W13]: +($C$158)
AI19 [C2 W13]: +($C$158)
AJ19 [C2 W13]: +($C$158)
AK19 [C2 W13]: +($C$158)
```

```
AL19 [C2 W13]: +($C$158)
AM19 [C2 W13]: +($C$158)
AN19 [C2 W13]: +($C$158)
AO19 [C2]:
AP19 [C2 W13]: @SUM(AC19..AN19)
AQ19 [C2]:
BA19: 'Press ALT-A for average over 100 calculations
BZ19: \-
CA19 [W12]: \-
CB19 [W12]: \-
CC19 [W12]: \-
CD19 [W12]: \-
CE19 [W12]: \-
CF19 [W12]: \-
CG19 [W12]: \-
CH19 [W12]: \-
CI19 [W12]: \-
CJ19 [W12]: \-
CK19 [W12]: \-
AA20: \-
AB20: \-
AC20 [W13]: \-
AD20 [W13]: \-
AE20 [W13]: \-
AF20 [W13]: \-
AG20 [C2 W13]: \-
AH20 [W13]: \-
AI20 [W13]: \-
AJ20 [W13]: \-
AK20 [W13]: \-
AL20 [W13]: \-
AM20 [W13]: \-
AN20 [W13]: \-
BZ20: 'Use ALT-S to store results
AA21: 'SUBTOTAL
AC21 [C2 W13]: @SUM(AC16..AC19)
AD21 [C2 W13]: @SUM(AD16..AD19)
AE21 [C2 W13]: @SUM(AE16..AE19)
AF21 [C2 W13]: @SUM(AF16..AF19)
AG21 [C2 W13]: @SUM(AG16..AG19)
AH21 [C2 W13]: @SUM(AH16..AH19)
AI21 [C2 W13]: @SUM(AI16..AI19)
AJ21 [C2 W13]: @SUM(AJ16..AJ19)
AK21 [C2 W13]: @SUM(AK16..AK19)
AL21 [C2 W13]: @SUM(AL16..AL19)
AM21 [C2 W13]: @SUM(AM16..AM19)
AN21 [C2 W13]: @SUM(AN16..AN19)
```

```
AP21 [C2 W13]: @SUM(AC21..AN21)
AA22: \-
AB22: \-
AC22 [W13]: \-
AD22 [W13]: \-
AE22 [W13]: \-
AF22 [W13]: \-
AG22 [W13]: \-
AH22 [W13]: \-
AI22 [W13]: \-
AJ22 [W13]: \-
AK22 [W13]: \-
AL22 [W13]: \-
AM22 [W13]: \-
AN22 [W13]: \-
AC23 [C2 W13]:
AN23 [C2 W13]:
AO23 [C2]:
AP23 [C2 W13]:
AQ23 [C2]:
AA24: \=
AB24: \=
AC24 [C2 W13]: \=
AD24 [C2 W13]: \=
AE24 [C2 W13]: \=
AF24 [C2 W13]: \=
AG24 [C2 W13]: \=
AH24 [C2 W13]: \=
AI24 [C2 W13]: \=
AJ24 [C2 W13]: \=
AK24 [C2 W13]: \=
AL24 [C2 W13]: \=
AM24 [C2 W13]: \=
AN24 [C2 W13]: \=
AO24 [C2]:
AP24 [C2 W13]:
AQ24 [C2]:
AA25: 'MONTHLY BALANCE
AC25 [C2 W13]: (AC11-AC21)
AD25 [C2 W13]: (AC25+AD11-AD21)
AE25 [C2 W13]: (AD25+AE11-AE21)
AF25 [C2 W13]: (AE25+AF11-AF21)
AG25 [C2 W13]: (AF25+AG11-AG21)
AH25 [C2 W13]: (AG25+AH11-AH21)
AI25 [C2 W13]: (AH25+AI11-AI21)
AJ25 [C2 W13]: (AI25+AJ11-AJ21)
AK25 [C2 W13]: (AJ25+AK11-AK21)
```

```
AL25 [C2 W13]: (AK25+AL11-AL21)
AM25 [C2 W13]: (AL25+AM11-AM21)
AN25 [C2 W13]: (AM25+AN11-AN21)
AO25 [C2]:
AP25 [C2 W13]:
AQ25 [C2]:
AA26: \=
AB26: \=
AC26 [C2 W13]: \=
AD26 [C2 W13]: \=
AE26 [C2 W13]: \=
AF26 [C2 W13]: \=
AG26 [C2 W13]: \=
AH26 [C2 W13]: \=
AI26 [C2 W13]: \=
AJ26 [C2 W13]: \=
AK26 [C2 W13]: \=
AL26 [C2 W13]: \=
AM26 [C2 W13]: \=
AN26 [C2 W13]: \=
AO26 [C2]:
AP26 [C2 W13]:
AQ26 [C2]:
AC47 [C2 W13]:
AN47 [C2 W13]:
AO47 [C2]:
AP47 [C2 W13]:
AQ47 [C2]:
AC48 [C2 W13]:
AN48 [C2 W13]:
AO48 [C2]:
AP48 [C2 W13]:
AQ48 [C2]:
A50: 'MACRO DATA
A51: '==========
A53: '{goto a100}~
C53: 'ALT-M GO TO MONTE CARLO DATA
G53: '{goto ca1}~
I53: 'ALT-P GO TO REPORT AREA
A55: '{goto aa1}~
C55: 'ALT-C GO TO CASHFLOW FORECAST
G55: 'ALT-S CREATE A REPORT AREA AND STORE VALUES
G56: '{goto ca6}~
J56: 0
K56: 'COUNTER 1
A57: '{goto a150}~
C57: 'ALT-D GO TO DEFAULT DATA
```

```
G57:  '{let j56,j56+1}~
J57:
K57:  'TOTAL SALES
G58:  '{let j60,+0}~
J58:
K58:  'TOTAL EXPENSES
A59:  '{goto a50}~
C59:  'ALT-K GO TO MACROS
G59:  '{let j60,j60+1}~
J59:
K59:  'EOY BALANCE
G60:  '{dn}~
J60:
K60:  'COUNTER 2
A61:  '{goto bal}~
C61:  'ALT-E GO TO DATA ENTRY SCREEN
G61:  '{if j60<j56}{jump g59}~
G62:  '/rcvbd4~~
J62:  'fix data
A63:  '{let bd3,+c202}~
C63:  'ALT-R RESTORE DEFAULT VALUES
G63:  '{rt}~
A64:  '{let bd4,+c203}~
G64:  '/rcvbd3~~
A65:  '{let bd5,+c205}~
G65:  '{rt}~
A66:  '{let bd6,+c206}~
G66:  '/rcvbd5~~
A67:  '{let bd7,+c207}~
G67:  '{rt}~
A68:  '{let bd8,+c209}~
G68:  '/rcvbd6~~
A69:  '{let bd9,+c210}~
G69:  '{rt}~
G70:  '/rcvbd7~~
A71:  'ALT-A AVERAGE BALANCE (100 CALCS)
G71:  '{rt}~
D72:
E72:  'COUNTER
G72:  '/rcvbd8~~
A73:  '{let d72,+0}~
D73:
E73:  'CUMULATIVE TOTAL
G73:  '{rt}~
A74:  '{let d73,+0}~
D74:
E74:  'AVERAGE
```

```
G74: '/rcvbd9~~
A75: '{blank bf6..bf6}~
G75: '{rt}~
A76: '{if d72=101}{jump a83}~
G76: '/rcvbf14~~
A77: '{calc}~
G77: '{rt}~
A78: '{let d72,d72+1}~
G78: '/rcvbf15~~
A79: '{let d73,d73+an25}~
G79: '{rt}~
A80: '{let bf7,'*COUNTING*}~
G80: '/rcvbf16~~
A81: '{let bf8,d72}~
G81: '{rt}~
A82: '{jump a76}~
G82: '/rcvbf6~~
A83: '{blank bf7..bf8}~
A84: '{let bf6,d73/100}~
A86: 'AUTOEXEC MACRO (SETS COUNTER TO ZERO FOR REPORT AREA)
A87: '{let j56,+0}~
H91 [F0]:
A100: 'LOOK UP TABLE
A101: '=============
A103: \-
B103: \-
C103: \-
D103: \-
E103: \-
F103: \-
G103: \-
H103: \-
I103: \-
J103: \-
K103: \-
A104: 'NO.
B104: ^1
C104: ^2
D104: ^3
E104: ^4
F104: ^5
G104: ^6
H104: ^7
I104: ^8
J104: ^9
K104: ^10
A105: \-
```

```
B105: \-
C105: \-
D105: \-
E105: \-
F105: \-
G105: \-
H105: \-
I105: \-
J105: \-
K105: \-
A106: 'PROB
B106: 0
C106: 5
D106: 10
E106: 25
F106: 45
G106: 60
H106: 75
I106: 80
J106: 85
K106: 90
A107: 'RATE
B107: 0.5
C107: 1
D107: 1.5
E107: 2
F107: 3
G107: 4
H107: 5
I107: 5.5
J107: 6
K107: 6.5
A108: \-
B108: \-
C108: \-
D108: \-
E108: \-
F108: \-
G108: \-
H108: \-
I108: \-
J108: \-
K108: \-
A110: 'SALES GROWTH
A111: '============
A113: 'MONTH
B113: ^JAN
```

```
C113: ^FEB
D113: ^MAR
E113: ^APRIL
F113: ^MAY
G113: ^JUNE
H113: ^JUL
I113: ^AUG
J113: ^SEPT
K113: ^OCT
L113: ^NOV
M113: ^DEC
A114: \-
B114: \-
C114: \-
D114: \-
E114: \-
F114: \-
G114: \-
H114: \-
I114: \-
J114: \-
K114: \-
L114: \-
M114: \-
A115: 'RAND.
B115: @INT(@RAND*100)+1
C115: @INT(@RAND*100)+1
D115: @INT(@RAND*100)+1
E115: @INT(@RAND*100)+1
F115: @INT(@RAND*100)+1
G115: @INT(@RAND*100)+1
H115: @INT(@RAND*100)+1
I115: @INT(@RAND*100)+1
J115: @INT(@RAND*100)+1
K115: @INT(@RAND*100)+1
L115: @INT(@RAND*100)+1
M115: @INT(@RAND*100)+1
A116: \-
B116: \-
C116: \-
D116: \-
E116: \-
F116: \-
G116: \-
H116: \-
I116: \-
J116: \-
```

```
K116: \-
L116: \-
M116: \-
A117: 'GROWTH
B117: @HTABLE((B115),$B$106..$K$107,1)
C117: @HTABLE((C115),$B$106..$K$107,1)
D117: @HTABLE((D115),$B$106..$K$107,1)
E117: @HTABLE((E115),$B$106..$K$107,1)
F117: @HTABLE((F115),$B$106..$K$107,1)
G117: @HTABLE((G115),$B$106..$K$107,1)
H117: @HTABLE((H115),$B$106..$K$107,1)
I117: @HTABLE((I115),$B$106..$K$107,1)
J117: @HTABLE((J115),$B$106..$K$107,1)
K117: @HTABLE((K115),$B$106..$K$107,1)
L117: @HTABLE((L115),$B$106..$K$107,1)
M117: @HTABLE((M115),$B$106..$K$107,1)
A118: \-
B118: \-
C118: \-
D118: \-
E118: \-
F118: \-
G118: \-
H118: \-
I118: \-
J118: \-
K118: \-
L118: \-
M118: \-
A150: 'STARTING VALUES FOR MEGAWIDGET CASHFLOW FORECAST
A151: '————————————————————
A152: 'SELLING PRICE
C152: +BD3
D152: '£
A153: 'STARTING SALES
C153: +BD4
D153: 'UNITS
A154: 'SALES GROWTH P.M.
C154: 5
D154: '% GIVING
E154: (C154/100)
A155: 'MATERIALS COST P.U.
C155: +BD5
D155: '£
A156: 'LABOUR COST P.U.
C156: +BD6
D156: '£
```

```
A157: 'POWER COST P.U.
C157: +BD7
D157: '£
A158: 'MONTHLY RENTAL
C158: 3000
D158: '£
A159: 'SAVINGS ACCOUNT
C159: +BD8
D159: '£
A160: 'INTEREST RATE P.A.
C160: +BD9
D160: '% - OR
E160: (C160/12)
F160: '% PER MONTH
D161: '  - GIVING
E161: (E160/100)
A163: 'Note: This area was retained from the original cashflow
forecast. It has
A164: 'now been altered so that values are taken from the data
entry screen.
A165: 'A new set of starting values (that cannot be altered) is
located
at A200.
A166: 'Additional (unnecessary) calculations are needed in the
worksheet - in
A167: 'an application created from scratch, this area would not
exist.
A200: 'STARTING VALUES FOR MEGAWIDGET CASHFLOW FORECAST
A201: '――――――――――――――――――――――――
A202: 'SELLING PRICE
C202: 9.99
D202: '£
A203: 'STARTING SALES
C203: 1000
D203: 'UNITS
A204: 'SALES GROWTH P.M.
C204: 5
D204: '% GIVING
E204: (C204/100)
A205: 'MATERIALS COST P.U.
C205: 5.75
D205: '£
A206: 'LABOUR COST P.U.
C206: 1.23
D206: '£
A207: 'POWER COST P.U.
C207: 0.77
```

```
D207: '£
A208: 'MONTHLY RENTAL
C208: 3000
D208: '£
A209: 'SAVINGS ACCOUNT
C209: 25000
D209: '£
A210: 'INTEREST RATE P.A.
C210: 12
D210: '% - OR
E210: (C210/12)
F210: '% PER MONTH
D211: '  - GIVING
E211: (E210/100)
A213: 'Note: These values can not be altered and are the 'true'
starting values
A214: 'for the cashflow forecast.
```

V. Data Table Example 1

```
A1 [W19]: 'AMOUNT:
B1 [C2 W12]: 20000
C1 [W15]: ' TERM:
D1 [W15]: 10
A2 [W19]: 'INTEREST RATE (PA):
B2 [%2 W12]: 0.05
C2 [W15]: ' EQUATION:
D2 [C2 W15]: @PMT(PRINCIPAL,INTEREST/12,TERM*12)
B5 [W12]: ^INTEREST RATE
C5 [W15]: ^PAYMENT
B6 [W12]: ^--------
C6 [W15]: ^----
C7 [C2 W15]: +D2
B8 [%2 W12]: 0.05
B9 [%2 W12]: 0.055
B10 [%2 W12]: 0.06
A11 [W19]: '******************
B11 [%2 W12]: 0.065
A12 [W19]: '* TABLE EXAMPLE 1 *
B12 [%2 W12]: 0.07
A13 [W19]: '******************
B13 [%2 W12]: 0.075
B14 [%2 W12]: 0.08
B15 [%2 W12]: 0.085
B16 [%2 W12]: 0.09
B17 [%2 W12]: 0.095
B18 [%2 W12]: 0.1
```

```
B19 [%2 W12]: 0.105
```

VI. Data Table Example 2

```
A1 [W19]: 'AMOUNT:
B1 [C2 W12]: 20000
C1 [W15]: ' TERM:
D1 [W15]: 10
A2 [W19]: 'INTEREST RATE (PA):
B2 [%2 W12]: 0.05
C2 [W15]: ' EQUATION:
D2 [C2 W15]: @PMT(PRINCIPAL,INTEREST/12,TERM*12)
B5 [W12]: ^INTEREST RATE
C5 [W15]: ^PAYMENT
B6 [W12]: ^————
C6 [W15]: ^———
B7 [W12]: +D2
C7 [W15]: 10
D7 [W15]: 15
E7 [W12]: 20
B8 [%2 W12]: 0.05
B9 [%2 W12]: 0.055
B10 [%2 W12]: 0.06
A11 [W19]: '*******************
B11 [%2 W12]: 0.065
A12 [W19]: '* TABLE EXAMPLE 1 *
B12 [%2 W12]: 0.07
A13 [W19]: '*******************
B13 [%2 W12]: 0.075
B14 [%2 W12]: 0.08
B15 [%2 W12]: 0.085
B16 [%2 W12]: 0.09
B17 [%2 W12]: 0.095
B18 [%2 W12]: 0.1
B19 [%2 W12]: 0.105
```

Appendix 5

Further Reading

The classic texts for competitive advantage are Michael Porter's *Competitive Advantage* and *Competitive Strategy*, both available world wide. However, the following general titles are offered as introductory texts for the areas covered by this book since they deal specifically with Information Technology.

Bodogli H., 1989, Decision Support Systems: Principles And Practice, West Publishing

Cashmore C. & Lyall R., 1991, Business Information Systems And Strategies, Prentice Hall

Curtis G., 1990, Business Information Systems: Analysis, Design and Practice, Addison-Wesley Publishers Ltd.

Ewing R., 1992, Introduction To Personal Computers, QUE

Firdman H., 1991, Strategic Information Systems, TAB

Stevens A., 1992, Teach Yourself Windows 3.1, M.I.S. Press

Sumner J., 1992, DOS 5 Quick Start Guide, Kuma